DIFFICULTIES IN LEARNING CAUSED BY TRAUMA

Anne Hurley
with Kathleen Grace

Published by
CoramBAAF Adoption and Fostering Academy
41 Brunswick Square
London WC1N 1AZ
www.corambaaf.org.uk

Coram Academy Limited, registered as a company limited by
guarantee in England and Wales number 9697712, part of the
Coram group, charity number 312278

Section I © Anne Hurley, 2021
Section II © Kathleen Grace, 2021

British Library Cataloguing in Publication Data
A catalogue record for this book is available from the British Library

ISBN 978 1 913384 14 2

Project management by Jo Francis, Publications Department,
CoramBAAF
Photograph on cover from www.istockphoto.com
Designed and typeset by Fravashi Aga
Printed in Great Britain by the Lavenham Press
Trade distribution by Turnaround Publisher Services, Unit 3,
Olympia Trading Estate, Coburg Road, London N22 6TZ

All rights reserved. Apart from any fair dealing for the purposes of
research or private study, or criticism or review, as permitted under
the Copyright, Designs and Patents Act 1988, this publication may
not be reproduced, stored in a retrieval system, or transmitted in
any form or by any means, without the prior written permission of
the publishers.

The moral rights of the authors have been asserted in accordance
with the Copyright, Designs and Patents Act 1988.

 For the latest news on CoramBAAF titles and special offers, sign up
to our free publications bulletin at https://corambaaf.org.uk/subscribe.

Contents

Looking behind the label…
Introduction												vii

SECTION I

UNDERSTANDING DIFFICULTIES IN LEARNING
### CAUSED BY TRAUMA									1

1. The importance of play for being able to learn						3
2. Ordinary learning at different stages of development					10
3. Difficulties in learning in the early years						22
4. Difficulties in learning in middle childhood						28
5. Difficulties in learning in adolescence						35
6. How to help										42

   Conclusion										54

SECTION II

PARENTING CHILDREN AFFECTED BY DIFFICULTIES
### IN LEARNING CAUSED BY TRAUMA							57

Our educational journey									59
Kathleen Grace

References										102
Useful CoramBAAF books									104
Useful organisations									106

Notes about the authors

Anne Hurley is a Consultant Child and Adolescent Psychotherapist at the Tavistock and Portman NHS Foundation Trust, where she leads the portfolio of psychoanalytic clinical and forensic training programmes. She previously worked in a specialist therapeutic service for fostered and adopted children in Enfield. She is a former social worker.

Kathleen Grace worked as a teacher for many years before choosing to become a single adopter. Brothers Shane and Ricky were placed together with her over 10 years ago. They were both already in primary school and displaying signs of having difficulty learning.

The series editor

Hedi Argent is an established author and editor. Her books cover a wide range of placement topics. She has written many guides and story books for young children.

Acknowledgements

I want to thank the long line of child psychotherapists at the Tavistock Clinic who helped me understand the emotional factors in learning and teaching, including Biddy Youell and Gillian Ingall. Grateful thanks too to all the foster carers, adoptive parents, children and young people who gave me insight into their experience over the years.
Anne Hurley

I am grateful to the readers of this manuscript, Sarah Borthwick and Ellie Johnson (Health Group Consultant, CoramBAAF), for their helpful comments. I am indebted to Jo Francis (Team Manager, CoramBAAF Publications) for her unfailing good humour and support throughout our work together on this series.
Hedi Argent

Looking behind the label…

Jack has mild learning difficulties and displays some characteristics of ADHD and it is uncertain whether this will increase…

Beth and Mary have diagnoses of global developmental delay…

Abigail's birth mother has a history of substance abuse. There is no clear evidence that Abigail was prenatally exposed to drugs but her new family will have to accept developmental uncertainty…

Jade has some literacy and numeracy difficulties, but has made some improvement with the support of a learning mentor…

Prospective adopters and carers are often faced with the prospect of having to decide whether they can care for a child with a health need or condition they know little about and have no direct experience of. No easy task…

Will Jack's learning difficulties become more severe?
Will Beth and Mary be able to catch up?
When will it be clear whether or not Abigail has been affected by parental substance misuse?
And will Jade need a learning mentor throughout her school life?

It can be difficult to know where to turn for reliable information. What lies behind the diagnoses and "labels" that many looked after children bring with them? And what will it be like to live with them? How will they benefit from family life?

Parenting Matters is a unique series, "inspired" by the terms used – and the need to "decode" them – in profiles of children needing new permanent families. Each title provides expert knowledge about a particular condition, coupled with facts, figures and guidance presented in a straightforward and accessible style. Each book also describes what it is like to parent an affected child, with either case studies or adopters and foster carers "telling it like it is", sharing their parenting experiences, and offering useful advice. This combination of expert information and first-hand experiences will help readers to gain understanding, and to make informed decisions.

Titles in the series deal with a wide range of health conditions and steer readers to where they can find more information. They offer a sound introduction to the topic under consideration and provide a glimpse of what it would be like to live with an affected child. Most importantly, this series looks behind the label and gives families the confidence to look more closely at a child whom they otherwise might have passed by.

Keep up with all our new books as they are published by signing up to our free publications bulletin at: https://corambaaf.org.uk/subscribe.

Titles in this series include:

- *Parenting a Child with ADHD*
- *Parenting a Child with Dyslexia*
- *Parenting a Child with Mental Health Issues*
- *Parenting a Child affected by Parental Substance Misuse*
- *Parenting a Child with Emotional and Behavioural Difficulties*
- *Parenting a Child with Autism Spectrum Disorder*
- *Parenting a Child with Developmental Delay*
- *Parenting a Child with, or at risk of, Genetic Disorders*
- *Parenting a Child affected by Domestic Violence*
- *Parenting a Child affected by Sexual Abuse*
- *Parenting a Child who has experienced Trauma*
- *Parenting a Child with Toileting Issues*
- *Parenting a Child with Eating and Food Issues*
- *Parenting a Child with Sleep Issues*

Introduction

Learning is an enriching experience when the mind is available for new knowledge and insight that can change who we are in the world. Engaging with this process, however, is fraught with complication, despite its apparent favourable promise. All learning happens in the context of a relationship and will therefore involve a broad range of emotions (Youell, 2006). Fundamentally, learning involves reliance on other people and acceptance that they have knowledge and wisdom to impart which we do not yet understand. Entering into a dependent learning relationship creates some ambivalence. Admiration, love and gratitude, as well as envy, resentment and competitiveness may be felt towards those sharing their knowledge and expertise. Anxiety is also likely to be experienced, as we struggle to understand something that feels just beyond reach, and being open to change by accommodating new ideas may not be straightforward.

Considerable frustration can be experienced when trying to

learn something that feels intangible and difficult to understand. Patience and tenacity are required to keep revisiting a topic that feels stubbornly obscure and beyond comprehension. There may be tedium in coping with the mundane business of foundational learning, like learning to spell long words and to recite times tables, but it becomes the gateway to higher-level knowledge. And then there are those moments of joyful epiphany when insight finally pings through the morass of uncertainty and confusion, sometimes on the back of much effort. The pleasure of deepening knowledge and understanding can be immensely satisfying, especially when care is taken to provide an inclusive environment that is respectful of differences in culture, race and ethnicity, gender, sexual orientation and religion. In formal education settings like schools, learning also involves assessment, judgement, monitoring and examination, tolerance of failure and success, and the range of emotional responses that accompany all of this. Learning is clearly an emotional process.

Learning starts early in life, and the way it is nourished or impeded has early origins. A highly influential psychoanalyst, Wilfred Bion, gave us a model of the mind that is predicated on the first relationship a baby forms with their mother, or indeed any other key adult who looks after the baby from birth. He described the transactional to-and-fro between baby and mother: the mother receives her baby's communications and interprets needs and wants in a highly sensitised transformative way, which leaves the baby feeling understood and contained. The cognitive effort of this processing, specifically inclined towards, and attuned to, the baby's needs, slowly begins to be internalised by the baby. Being thought about with love and concern allows the beginnings of a thinking mind to emerge, an internal space to make sense of and to process experience (Bion, 1962). It is within this first relationship that all learning starts, and it has long-lasting effects.

These early foundations of learning are easily disrupted by the absence of a loving, attentive adult in infancy. In situations of severe neglect, trauma or abuse, there is little sense of a baby being sufficiently contained or held in mind by a caring adult who has their interests clearly at heart. The baby's mind is left overwhelmed by sensations and unmediated terrors that cannot be processed. For protection, babies form defensive barriers like zoning out, cutting off and shutting down. In so doing, they are trying to keep out intolerable levels of anxiety, but the corollary of these defensive measures is that their mind is not available for learning. There is little receptivity to what's on offer in the external world when that world has become equated with hostility, threat and traumatic intrusion. Emotional barriers to learning can be entrenched and persist well into childhood and beyond, even when the original adverse situation has long been replaced with a more caring environment and by thoughtful carers. This can be dispiriting, yet every effort by a consistent, dependable adult matters. Children need adopters, foster carers, teachers and social workers around them who can think about their experience and give it meaning and coherence. Cumulative efforts over time by caring adults, to think about and find ways of overcoming obstacles to learning, tilt children in a more hopeful orientation towards new learning possibilities.

This book does not address learning difficulty that has its origins in congenital disability or neurological disorders like ADHD (attention deficit hyperactivity disorder) or dyslexia. The focus instead is on learning problems that emerge in the context of disruptive early relationships, neglect and trauma, which interfere with the process of ordinary learning. Learning, in this context, is not restricted to academic work in school, but includes more ordinary life skills that develop or are hindered depending on the kind of circumstances in which children grow up.

SECTION I

UNDERSTANDING DIFFICULTIES IN LEARNING CAUSED BY TRAUMA

ANNE HURLEY

CHAPTER 1

The importance of play for being able to learn

This chapter on play is included in this book because play is fundamental to learning. Children learn about themselves, their relationships and their world by playing. Some examples of play from babyhood through to childhood are described below to show how play can be a subtle but crucial spur to learning and development.

Play is associated with pleasurable free time, but is sometimes demoted to a secondary activity that happens during breaks away from the more centrally important formal learning in the classroom setting. However, free play and learning are increasingly understood as closely and mutually linked. Play is essential developmental and creative work that facilitates and promotes learning in all kinds of subtle and more explicit ways. It provides opportunities for enjoyable exploration and imaginative experimentation that support emotional, cognitive and neurological development. Play activities involve dexterity and physical skill as well as energetic fun, so that motor development is stretched. Play can be a solitary occupation that develops the capacity for being productively alone, or a more sociable pursuit that advances relationships with others in a collaborative way.

When playing with others, how to share toys and play equipment has to be worked out. The direction of play scenarios and roles, although malleable, need rough agreement as they unfold. Playing involves negotiation, the art of persuasion, sorting out problems with others in pairs and in groups, as well as learning to manage and recover from conflict. Group activities and team sports provide opportunities for self-promotion and leadership as well as for yielding and following other people's lead, and that means learning about social relationships from different angles. Experiences of belonging and fitting in are valued, and experiences of being left out and excluded are suffered. Through play, friendships are established and sustained and companionable industry is enjoyed. Play advances complex communication, and develops social competence.

Early play in babyhood

Initial play is in the context of the interaction between babies and their loving carers. Early games incorporate imitation and taking turns, like clapping along to rhyming songs, each taking up their part at the appropriate juncture. Close observation and attention are nurtured in such games while a deepening emotional connection is also being made. Games like "Heads, shoulders, knees and toes" encourage bodily self-awareness and make links between the verbal naming and corresponding identification of body areas by touch. Small accomplishments are met with acclaim and much pleasure, the precursor of rewards for getting something right later. Some play has the benefit of learning to regulate arousal levels. A game of "Round and round the garden", for instance, deliberately escalates arousal levels through the pleasure of anticipated tickling, before restoring calm and starting all over again. Generating different registers of stimulation in this way introduces excitement, but not enough to make it overwhelming. The baby is being taught about the ups and downs of different emotional states in an atmosphere of shared enjoyment. The attention span is also lengthened by repetition – always important for learning. "Peek-a-boo" is an early game with representational importance. It involves transitory hiding and re-discovery, sometimes with feigned amplified anxiety marking the "disappearance" and exuberant celebration at the "return". It supports the idea that the person momentarily out of sight is still there and will come back. This spurs on the beginnings of internal representation and abstraction, as well as being a miniature rehearsal for loss associated with separation.

These kinds of games in babyhood have not come about by design with the intention of imparting skills. There is no educative curriculum, nor an agenda for formal learning operating here. They have emerged organically on the carer's lap, in the spirit of companionable fun and loving mutual enjoyment. The development and the support for speech and language are simply by-products of play.

Toddlers learning through play

Growing independence means that play without the facilitation of adults becomes more possible in young childhood. Play takes on a more self-directed quality, with toddlers as agents taking charge of what happens as they explore the world around them. Objects are examined closely, blocks are put one on top of the other in a construction that then is roughly felled. Buckets are filled and emptied and filled up again. Toy trains go on journeys along tracks. There is interest in putting objects together and understanding how they potentially connect and come apart in the industry of co-ordination. There is engagement with different shapes, sensory qualities, colours and patterns: the beginnings of scientific discovery. Individual preferences can be exercised as to how long any one toy is played with, quickly discarded or placed at the beginning of a sequence that develops over time. Choosing activities of one's own volition imparts confidence and some feeling of self-determination. There is also interest in what peers are doing: observation of their play takes concentration, and is a preparation for later joining in.

Learning through symbolic play

Symbolic play brings further complexity. The possibility of playing house and having the role of mummy or daddy, or being the nursery leader, teacher, doctor or supermarket cashier, is a way of processing daily experience, and potentially anticipating changes in daily activities. What happens is now self-directed and there is a chance of taking bearings from a range of different positions and viewpoints, including from within the adult world. Trying out different roles in play is not a replica of life experience, but a medley of scraps of direct experience, shot through with imaginings from inner thoughts and feelings. The narrative of what is being enacted is fluid and imaginative and provides a different perspective on life events, both real and in fantasy. Playing at being mummy having a baby, or being the doctor helping deliver a new baby in the hospital, for example, provide new ways of viewing the arrival of a baby sibling in the family. The assignation of a role with more power in the proceedings than the child naturally has may alleviate fears of being usurped by a rival child. In this new scenario, someone else can be the recipient of ambivalent feelings about a new baby brother or sister. Playing at being the cross teacher bossing the class around for not getting their work done, may place feelings of anxiety and fear about learning and harsh treatment at nursery or school elsewhere for a time. These are meaningful stories being played out, and they are an aid to learning how to process emotional experience.

The storylines in children's play often include "magical thinking". A person may be obliterated in a horrendous car crash, driven to hospital and pronounced dead by the doctor and come back to life again, fully recovered, moments later. Imaginative play regularly contains scenes of considerable aggression and violence: shocking scenes featuring devastating battles, bloody annihilations, heads shot off, dead babies, poisonous injections, mass murders. Rescue missions are also launched with fire engines, ambulances and police being brought into service.

Children know that play is the arena in which to give vent to all kinds of survival anxieties and destructiveness without anyone actually getting attacked, hurt or dying. It is a way of expressing and working through underlying conflicts and anxieties in young childhood without coming to harm or doing harm. If destructive urges are expressed and located in the fantasy world of play, it frees children up to some extent for more cordial relationships in the external world. It may also help create more space in the mind for some of the learning tasks in formal education, which require calm attention and concentration.

Children who need help to play

Children who have not had sufficient experience of loving, playful transactions as babies and young children struggle to play and do not know how to join in with a play activity. They are simply unable to play, and this is likely to be noticeable in nursery and school. They may remain on the outskirts, quietly appearing self-sufficient and untroubled, when really they are lost or cut off. Alternatively, they may be energetically rushing around, loudly disruptive, unable to regulate mood and behaviour, requiring a great deal of adult help to settle. Neglected and emotionally deprived children may go through the motions of playing but without passionate engagement or evident enjoyment. Their play is often stunted and restricted, or gets stuck in repetitive, stale, short sequences, which are never extended or elaborated. This is dulling for the mind and lacks the vital creativity necessary for healthy development.

CASE STUDY

Teachers in six-year-old Jake's primary school noticed that he struggled at free playtime and was often alone in the playground. They observed other children trying to interest him in joining their games, but he seemed oblivious of their efforts. For instance, a ball directed to him would be ignored as if he had no concept of the back and forth of a football game, and so other children soon gave up on him.

His school provided a structured opportunity for him to play with another child, supervised by a teaching assistant showing him what to do and giving him a great deal of praise when he joined in. Slowly, he came a little more alive and was able to participate without active encouragement and direct instruction.

Jake's withdrawal had developed in the context of his first five years spent trying to avoid the negative attention of his stepfather who regularly physically abused him. It was safer for him to stay in the background. Only slowly did a united effort by his teachers and foster carers help him to come out of the shadows and realise that joining in does not risk harm. His confidence also became more evident in the classroom, as he gradually was able to participate in phonic games to help him learn to read.

Usually, children are able to clearly differentiate between the fantasy world of pretend play and the actual world. However, severely traumatised children may seriously struggle with this and experience confusion and collisions between what is real and what is not, which may make play a muddling, if not frightening, prospect.

CASE STUDY

Four-year-old Assad became absolutely distraught when a girl at his table in nursery began driving a toy ambulance to hospital, telling her companions that the mummy was very sick and needed an operation.

Assad's earlier experience in a war-torn country had involved him witnessing scenes of horrific injury and lots of exposure to emergency services. He was all mixed up about what was real and what was imaginary. His nursery worker had to reassure him that this was just pretend play and no one actually needed to go to hospital.

A child who cannot play is likely to be functioning at a cognitive level that is concerning, and will need concerted help to move towards genuine playfulness that spurs on learning.

CHAPTER 2

Ordinary learning at different stages of development

In order to understand the learning difficulties children may face, it is important to understand the "ordinary" learning process at different ages. Awareness of the range of learning that happens in normal circumstances as children grow up provides a baseline against which to explore what traumatised children may not have been able to learn.

Early learning

Babies come into the world primed to learn, as they adjust to the world outside their mother's body. Disoriented from the shock of birth, they are faced with new sensations, sounds, smells, space, and experience bright light, air and gravity for the first time. There is a much-changed environment to encounter. In the womb, feeding was automatic, so unsurprisingly early learning is centered on forming a feeding relationship. Newborn babies' interest is focused on finding their way to the breast or bottle, putting their sucking reflex to good use, looking at their mother's face and getting to know her in a new intimate closeness. Life on the lap is not only about feeding, it is also about playing and "chatting", and exploring within the confines of safe arms. The soothing of loving touch and close physical holding is key to babies forming close and secure attachments. Bodily discomfort and dissatisfaction are communicated in no uncertain terms by howling cries. Parents and carers absorb and interpret this distress and do what they can to find its source: hunger, wind, soiled nappy, need for company, and they act to remedy and restore calm as much as possible. Babies' early frustrations are fraught with fear and hard to bear, they have an urgency and intensity that demand immediate attention. Over time, the raw distress lessens and babies can manage a little more dissatisfaction for a little longer.

Learning away from the lap

When the foundation of loving connection with reliable parents or carers is in place, babies become more able to be on their own for a little while, and this opens up new learning opportunities. There is the world of objects to explore. Holding a rattle can produce sounds, reaching for and pushing a soft toy hanging on the cot results in its swinging movement. The discovery of agency is experienced, the delight of being able to make things happen: in essence, learning about cause and effect. Parental endorsement of these small developmental achievements instills confidence to continue exploration. Physical development – crawling away, learning to stand, recovering from falls, cruising around furniture and taking first steps – allows further new discovery. Buttons to press on noisy toys, boxes to upend and bang on, cupboards to explore and empty, are all available for research. Such experimentation is interspersed with retreat to a parent figure for reassurance and physical comfort before another foray away.

Learning to communicate

Babies have language and sound around them from the beginning. They are familiar with the voices of their mother and father or close others, and derive comfort and reassurance from hearing them. During their first year, babies move from babbling to playing with sounds and putting strings of different sounds together. This learning does not happen in a solitary way, but in the context of a relationship, a reciprocal exchange of long, babbling sociable chats with playful intonation and pitch. Early interaction is crucial for brain development and has long-lasting consequences, as Gerhardt (2004) explores in her book, *Why Love Matters*. A loving relationship from birth sets the baby on a path to optimal neurological development.

Parenting includes the important function of setting boundaries. The word "no" features in conversations and babies understand that limits are being placed on them, a recognition that is not without vocal protest on occasion. Learning to imitate utterances and gestures brings mutual enjoyment between babies and their parents or carers. Pointing at something as a way of indicating what is needed, and being understood with responsiveness, instils a sense of personal power and self-importance when the object of desire arrives, delivered by a person who understood the communication. In ordinary family life, first words spark a celebratory atmosphere, and babies enjoy being the centre of much praise and positive regard. It is a motivating push forward to learn more.

Introducing books

Reading books together in the early years, with a young child in the lap of a parent or carer, introduces a new experience of language: the written word with accompanying pictures. Looking at books together spurs on speech and language development and the beginnings of literacy. Parents and carers often naturally supply an additional narrative alongside the text in the picture book, capturing the young child's interest and engagement. There is animated drama involved in story time. Simple tasks like finding the bear in a complex picture, for example, go alongside the main storyline. This is fun, but it also means searching through complex visual information to identify the bear. This kind of scanning involves attending to a particular task and marks the beginnings of learning to concentrate for a short spell of time. The brain is at work. Emotional development is also fostered as patience, perseverance and capacity to tolerate frustration are encouraged in micro-doses, when the quest for the bear is not immediately successful. And, of course, there is pleasure when the bear is finally pointed out and success is marked with applause.

Young children who have the experience of being read to in this way will be naturally introduced to "question and answer" sessions: 'Where's the doggy gone?' They begin to learn about object constancy. The dog has not disappeared, he is behind the flap on the page with the picture of the park, which can be opened and closed at will – bringing to mind yesterday's real-life visit to the park further connects up different elements of experience. The pleasure of reading a favourite book, again and again, establishes the sequence of the story, and builds up anticipation and memory. Often books for young children present visual images that can be counted and colour-coded. They give opportunities for categorisation: 'Let's find all the red flowers in the picture, let's see how many we can find'. What is at play here are the subtle roots of cognitive organisation. Literacy and numeracy skills are being slowly nurtured with adult oversight and mediation. The foundation of later learning is being established. In addition, the emotional tasks of the under-five period are being addressed.

The content of popular books for this age group so often tackles key challenges and conflicts, which serve to process emotional experience. For example, Max goes on a rampage of fury and rebellion, but manages to find his way back to a warm supper in *Where the Wild Things Are* (Sendak, 1963). It conveys the positive message that "monstrousness" can be tamed and there is a recovery from rage. Another popular book, *We're Going on a Bear Hunt*, is a story of overcoming head-on fear-inducing obstacles on an adventurous journey (Rosen and Oxenbury, 1989). It encourages courage and forbearance in the face of new experiences, yet another helpful lesson. Many other stories tackle issues to do with getting lost and being found again, separation and reunion, which is fruitful psychological preparation for time to come spent outside the family context.

Learning in middle childhood

Middle childhood in primary school is a relatively calm period in comparison with the intensity of feelings associated with the early years. It comes before the revival of inner conflict and emotional upheaval with the start of adolescence. Middle childhood is a period sometimes known as "latency", as some of the passions associated with the early years have largely been laid to rest. Close family relationships remain crucial, but there is more orientation outward and away from the family.

Starting school

Children first encountering school are likely to have had some earlier experience of being in a nursery or other child-care setting, where managing periods outside their family home has already been established. Most will have had exposure to different skin colours, cultures, accents and religions, and will have some knowledge and appreciation of societal diversity. Although there is a huge variation of experience, by the time children start school they are normally enjoying some degree of independence and autonomy. For example, they are usually able to eat and dress without help, and they are used to going to the toilet by themselves. More dependency needs, or upset expressed by

Ordinary learning at different stages of development

tummy pains and perhaps occasional toileting accidents, may emerge at times of stress, but largely these are transitory.

All children now grow up in a digital environment, and so will have some familiarity with technology and are likely to be able to use a tablet or computer. They can probably count and know the alphabet. They may remember rhymes and sing songs. If looking at books is an enjoyable experience, they may recognise letters, some written words and perhaps their own name. Some children start school already able to read and write basic short sentences; others will be complete beginners, but can hold a pencil and make rudimentary drawings and copy simple shapes.

The pace of emotional and social development is never uniform. However, the chances are that sitting at a table, taking turns, waiting for a while without gratification, not always having needs met, and sharing with others are all familiar experiences. Latency-aged children are able to express themselves and communicate their wishes and needs clearly. They are sociable, interested in making friends, more usually, though not exclusively, same-sex friends at this stage. They often have a best friend and navigate their way in peer groups reasonably well, though with some adult refereeing of disputes. Following the instructions of authoritative adults is an ordinary part of daily life. Before going to "big school", their relationships with parents/carers, grandparents and other adults in caring roles will have been generally positive. This sets the scene for the expectation that teachers, similarly, will be helpful people, who will be interested in their welfare. They come to school, perhaps with some anxiety about the newness of it all. They may at first feel quite lost and bewildered, but they have been prepared by facilitating adults, or perhaps an older brother or sister, and so have some idea of what to expect. Optimism and excitement consequently dampen down some of the worry associated with this new chapter in life outside the home.

Helpfulness of school routines

School life provides structures and routines within which to learn. This makes the busyness and noise of the classroom more manageable. Timetables measure out the day. Teachers follow the curriculum. There are rules, regulations and clarity about boundaries, and what behaviour is expected and what incurs sanctions. Fairness and the application of rules in an equitable way are important, as latency-aged children often have a strong sense of right and wrong and can be vehement advocates of justice. Environmental issues like climate change and causes to do with animal welfare are among the many campaigns that can capture children's strong allegiance and advocacy in primary school. Some pursue such causes with passionate dedication, wanting to make a difference and do good in the world. Children at this stage often want the responsibility of looking after a pet.

Learning in primary school

The primary school years are so much about acquiring knowledge and new skills. Learning to ride a bike or scooter, racing, chasing and climbing, becoming adept at dance, football or other sports, all promote physical development and co-ordination. They are also years of industry, concentration, amassing lots of information, planning and problem-solving. Construction and craft projects and virtual games like *Minecraft* that provide simulated worlds away from adults are popular. Children become proficient at rote learning, reeling off times tables for instance, and accumulate masses of factual information. Work is geared to achieve the key stages expected at various points in primary school, and taking tests becomes routine. All learning involves tolerating making mistakes and coping with not understanding. There is inevitable frustration as well as excitement when the dawn of insight breaks through. Results in standard attainment tests (SATs) may not always be as hoped for. Accepting setbacks and patient persistence allows literacy and numeracy to slowly and progressively develop. It is not uncommon for children to get fed up and irritable on occasion, and to resist their teacher's instructions. However, the major "meltdowns" of the early years are past; praise and positive reinforcement are usually effective, and generally moodiness and disobedience are weathered without significant eruptions.

Canham (2006) reminds us that not all aggression disappears during the latency years, but it is more likely to find expression in healthy competition. Winning games, being chosen for the best roles in the school play or concert, being on the winning side in a football match, or being the one selected by the teacher for some esteemed classroom task, all take on an importance. Collecting is a common activity during primary school years, whether it is Pokémon cards, football stickers, fidget spinners or the latest playground craze. Collections open up comparative discussions with friends, and having a rare item can elevate a child's popularity. Duplicate items are swapped and skills in bartering and negotiation are developed.

The beginning of puberty

A new consciousness of the body emerges with the onset of puberty and the associated swarm of physical changes. There is a wide variation in when this begins. Some girls have to contend with the start of menstruation at primary school, others not until secondary school. Similarly, boys will vary in age in terms of their physical development. Towards the end of the primary school years, the move towards adolescence becomes apparent.

Learning in adolescence

The dual difficulty of adapting to the challenges of secondary school and coping with the bodily preoccupations that puberty brings, while not necessarily concurrent for all young people, makes early adolescence a complex time. Physically, the body is going through a period of rapid change and hormonal fluctuation.

Boys are producing semen, experiencing wet dreams, coping with changes in voice and the emergence of facial hair. Girls' bodies are changing with the development of breasts and start of menstruation. Although, physiologically, pregnancy is possible, emotional readiness for becoming a parent lags far behind. Psychologically, there is a wish for greater independence, a more ambivalent relationship with parental figures, a questioning of personal identity, the establishment of a sexual identity, and a transition to life that is more apart from the family context.

The turbulence of adolescence

Adolescence is a time marked by internal turbulence, confusion and extremes of mood. Time passing and the loss of childhood are unavoidable. During adolescence, the security provided by a stable home life remains an important anchor, although there may be ostensible opposition to and expressed disdain for it from the young person. Parents and carers are often made to feel deficient, redundant and an embarrassing surplus, while their interest, involvement and consistent authority are covertly still very much required.

The impact of racism on young people

Young people from minority ethnic groups are likely to experience additional pressures in adolescence. Spending more time outside the family will bring new awareness of being potentially viewed through a racist lens, with the associated risks and threats. Black young people are over-represented in police "stop and search" statistics in the UK, and being prepared to submit to this intrusiveness by a person of power and authority is highly stressful, especially when evidence of suspicion is absent and it is felt to be grossly unfair. Anger at racial injustice often goes unexpressed, although the Black Lives Matter campaign has provided space to highlight and voice the prevalence of racism and its impact. Anger, when turned inward, takes its toll on young people. Experiences of casual racist abuse on the streets, in parks and at school persist, and anxieties about injustice and attack are weathered at some emotional cost.

Finding a place at secondary school

Transfer to secondary school requires an adjustment to being the youngest again in an unfamiliar, often large institution. New students have to get used to a number of different teachers, and will probably have to move to different classrooms for different subjects along corridors with lots of noise and jostling, which can be daunting. It may be a frightening and anxiety-provoking adaptation. The task of finding a place in a friendship group is another challenge and may initially involve a period of instability, uncertainty and loneliness, especially if links with friends from primary school are severed. Group life is an immersive experience during the secondary school years, and a sense of belonging to a group with similar values and interests provides a safe place to explore identity and experiment with new ways of being. Groups converge around shared music, fashion, alternate fantasy worlds like animé or manga, social activism or political ideologies, and this may be all-consuming for the young person.

Waddell (2018) describes group membership as having a "holding function" for adolescents, a safe place for reworking and integrating aspects of self, including residual infantile fears and conflicts. Group life can also be a source of intense anxiety, with fluidity of group hierarchy and membership, shifting allegiances and rivalries, and feelings of betrayal and being left out all making for a complicated group existence. In this digital age, group life is conducted online as well as in person. Online contact with friends became especially important during the 2020/21 Covid-19 pandemic lockdowns, when meeting face-to-face was not possible. The age of 13 marks the point when young people are officially allowed membership of popular social media platforms such as Facebook, although many are digitally active long before. This confers quasi-adult status in a new way, but it may also feel like a very pressurised public space in which to operate. The emphasis on approval of physical appearance and acceptance based on the number of "likes" for social media postings can make emotional well-being a rather precarious commodity.

Sexual identity

There may also be pressure on young people to become sexually active earlier than they feel ready, borne out of competitiveness or a perception about fitting in, rather than genuinely felt desire. The prevalence of online pornography, available at a young age, distorts the nature of ordinary sexual relationships. The beginnings of becoming sexual, whatever the orientation, can be fraught with uncertainty and anxiety, but adult sexuality represented in pornography can further complicate the path to sexual experimentation in a way that is respectful and consensual. It is important that this is countered by open discussion at home, and in sex and relationship education in school.

Preparing for exams

Adolescence marks a time of significant neurological development and rapid cognitive change. There is a shift to more sophisticated abstract thinking and creativity, analytic appraisal of ideas, evaluation of differing perspectives on a wide range of issues, and a capacity to take up a personal position with a reasoned argument, perhaps passionately made. Young people aged 14–16 in England and Wales are working at Key Stage 4 (S5 in Scotland) towards national qualifications, usually GCSEs in England and Wales (National 5 Qualifications in Scotland), and the approach of these exams can galvanise them to study and revise in preparation. However, there may also be a range of different responses to this hurdle. Some adolescents may feign a "don't care" attitude to mask a fear of failure. Others may feel pressure to deny the extent of their private study if it is out of alignment with the peer group's disaffected posturing about formal education. This first state exam can also pose an unconscious conflict: to want the same thing as parents or carers, namely, to achieve good results, while simultaneously being emotionally invested in being different to and separate from them. Exam success may feel centrally important as a step towards assuming responsibility for direction in adult life. It marks a potential point of leaving school with some qualifications or a significant punctuation point en route to continuing education.

CHAPTER **3**

Difficulties in learning in the early years

Following on from the last chapter, which looked at learning in ordinary family circumstances, this chapter turns to difficulties with learning that children who are adopted or fostered may experience.

Babies come into the world ready to relate to other people and curious about the world around them. When babies do not feel held and contained, loved, nourished and sheltered, and do not have their needs met in early life, brain development is unsupported and the conditions for learning are not set in a helpful direction. Learning is all about taking in, absorbing, working over the unfamiliar in the mind, often with a supportive adult in attendance. If a positive feeding relationship, which is associated with reciprocal understanding and satisfaction, has not been established, then the receptivity associated with learning will also not be established for the child.

Difficulties in learning in the early years

When babies and young children have not had the benefit of sustained, helpful, nourishing early relationships, as is the case for many children who have been in care, then there are likely to be some emotional barriers to learning. Periods of lengthy abandonment and neglect, marked inconsistency of care or sudden intrusive experiences interrupt the process of ordinary receptivity. If feeding has not been a benign, satisfying process, but was tinged with negativity and overshadowed by threat or fear of survival, then infants and young children will be prone to intolerable anxiety and will protect themselves as much as possible with defensive measures. They may become quite cut off or shut down, and regularly "disappear" in dissociative states. Dissociation is a way for the mind to cope with excessive stress. It involves a feeling of disconnection that is more than an ordinary lapse of attention, and can include not being sure of who you are, forgetting periods of time and events, and not feeling pain. Young children who are dissociated may seem quiet, and their quietness may give the surface appearance of being "good". They are not oriented outwards, and are likely to need active "reclaiming" in order to be able to learn.

CASE STUDY

Eighteen-month-old Amy, whose first year was spent with a young mother who had depression and who failed to muster much interest in her, was failing to thrive. Her foster carer described her going through the motions of eating and playing, but something about her was essentially vacant and lifeless. Her speech development was delayed and she was passive, withdrawn and uninterested in her surroundings for the majority of the time. It took sustained proactive attention by her foster carer over many months

> to ignite her interest in interacting and making eye contact, but even then she easily retreated to a default position of withdrawal.

Many young children who are now fostered or adopted, following abusive experiences in early life, will be assailed by emotional states that are impossible for them to process. These usually persist long after the actual danger has passed and are often discharged through restlessness, agitation and behavioural disturbance. Consequently, availability for learning is severely curtailed.

CASE STUDIES

Four-year-old Kevin was defiant, unsettled and aimlessly flitted from one activity to another in nursery. He could not concentrate. He had seemingly random aggressive tantrums and he hit and hurt other children. He had been exposed to domestic abuse in his first two years, and had signs of old injuries when he was removed from his birth home. He often, suddenly and violently, shook the shared small table at nursery and enacted earthquakes with the dolls' house, shaking it precariously, close to destruction. He forcefully conveyed that he knew about houses that could rock into violent action at any point. He was now unwittingly re-enacting something of his earlier childhood in a way that kept feelings of fear and vulnerability at bay.

Three-year-old Hitesh was in a similar predicament, having sustained physical and sexual abuse at the hands of his step-father and having received little protection from his mother. He was causing havoc at nursery, regularly upending tables and throwing books at other children. He had had a few different foster placements and was now living with prospective adopters, with whom he was beginning to forge a good connection. When he was playing with a toy train, he told his adoptive mother that his train was moving on wobbly tracks. This was a graphic image, communicating his sense of a life always on the brink of derailment, not rooted or belonging anywhere.

Communication via behaviour, not words

Kevin and Hitesh were unconsciously communicating through their actions and behaviour some of the disturbance emanating from traumatic early experience. They had no words for what had happened. Children under five are commonly characterised by progressively improving emotional regulation, albeit with lapses that need adult mediation. Normally, tantrums are less frequent and intense as the years pass and starting school approaches. However, children in circumstances like Amy, Kevin and Hitesh have not had the kind of foundation that would help them to regulate their feelings. Their self-control is uncertain and prone to disintegration with little provocation. Their speech and language development, especially in the cases of Amy and Kevin, lags behind that of their chronological peers. However, there is hope. They now have adults in their lives who are actively trying to understand how their children are revealing troubling experiences. They are trying to understand the meaning of behaviour, as well as putting firm boundaries around it, which is helping the children to feel a little more contained and available for new learning.

Difficulty with separation

The capacity to bear some separation away from parents or carers is an achievement usually associated with the early years. Internal resources are slowly constructed through serial good experiences of mindful care that make separation more manageable. There is the slow internalising of a helpful "parental figure" that can be sustaining when the actual parent is not present. However, when care is inconsistent, haphazard, neglectful or unpredictably traumatic, the mind's internal architecture cannot develop a specifically helpful figure. Instead, there may be internal tormentors who, instead of giving reassurance, offer malign suggestions that the child is bad and worthless. Young children may fear that they are so bad that no one will ever be able to stay with them. It makes separation from a foster carer or adopter very difficult if the young child unconsciously believes that they will not be collected from nursery at the end of the day.

Gaps in early care and impact on learning

Adverse experience in the early years is connected with delayed emotional development. In the absence of consistent, reliable loving care, struggles with emotional regulation and separation anxiety may persist for longer than would be expected, given the child's chronological age. Ordinary early childhood games that extend attention and concentration, and exploring story books in adult company that advance communication skills and facilitate the beginnings of literacy and numeracy, are more likely to be a scarce commodity in emotionally deprived circumstances. Cognitive, speech and language development are then also compromised, with negative consequences for learning. Moreover, self-care skills like washing, dressing and toileting may not have been learned if these areas were neglected or given scant regard in the early years. This can lead to children having negative experiences at home, school and in other environments, and therefore not being open to learning.

Additionally, models of internalised relationships may be infused with violence, denigration, humiliation and manipulation, because this is what children's early experiences have taught them to expect. This is a problematic template from which to develop peer relationships and collaborative links with teachers and other educational staff. In many ways, then, young children who have experienced a background of neglect or trauma approach the start of formal learning, when they begin school, with significant disadvantages. Some are unlikely to achieve great grades as they have a number of emotional impediments to learning to overcome in order to succeed at school.

CHAPTER **4**

Difficulties in learning in middle childhood

The transition to primary school marks a key punctuation point for every child, perhaps tinctured with both excitement and nervousness. This new milestone may bring hope and expectation, but it can be daunting and bewildering to enter "big school". Youell (2006), in writing about education from a psychoanalytic perspective, describes every new start as involving anxiety about confronting the unknown. She writes about transitions evoking 'memories about other losses and earlier fearful beginnings'. For children who have been removed from their birth families, perhaps in crisis, or who have experienced a number of different foster placements in their young lives, the memories that may be evoked can be particularly complicated. There may be echoes of leaving birth parents, and anxiety and guilt about the welfare of family members left behind, and memories of being forcibly removed from the only situation that was familiar, despite its traumatic nature. Children who have had previous foster placement or adoption breakdowns may well have memories reawakened that are associated with fears about rejection. Therefore, it is likely that children who have a traumatic, fragmented past with lots of change may take longer to settle into school. It may be particularly important for them to have thoughtful preparation in advance, including opportunities to visit the new school, meet their teacher and gain some foresight about what to expect.

Potential problems adjusting to school

The adjustment period for starting primary school may coincide with more neediness and clinginess at home, upsets and bouts of tearfulness, and physical complaints like tummy pains and sleeping problems. As a foster carer or adopter, your emotional support will be crucial for your child in weathering the transition to school, and indeed other smaller transitions like returning to school after half-term or beginning a new academic year. It is not uncommon for children to present quite differently in different contexts (for example, at home and at school), which is not a reflection of either situation meeting the child's needs better. It may be that there is increased disturbance in the home setting, which can feel barely containable, because that is where the child feels safest to express anxieties, whereas at school they are seemingly managing the new challenges of formal learning.

Many children who have experienced neglect and trauma in their early lives are able to make good use of what is on offer at school, and it may provide relieving respite from the intimacy of family life. The clarity around school rules and regulations are helpful parameters. The ordinary routines and structures associated with school life can feel nurturing and holding. The rhythm of the school day, working on prescribed tasks in an assigned place in the classroom, punctuated by set break times and lining up for lunch, has a predictable pattern that provides stability and containment. Less structured playground time may be more problematic for children who have not had secure early relationships. They may feel lost, socially unskilled and anxious. They are likely to need adult help in establishing friendships and joining in games. Teachers, teaching assistants and other school staff who are able to listen to pupils' concerns and are fair and kind in their approach, can be a supportive presence.

Specific issues with formal learning for fostered or adopted children

However, some children who are fostered or adopted really flounder at school. If they have shut down their emotional availability to protect themselves from the full impact of earlier neglect or abuse, then any learning will be difficult. If children find it emotionally troubling to make a mistake, equating any imperfect work with a catastrophe and confirmation of their worthlessness, then they may be tempted to give up. This may seem easier than meeting self-imposed, impossibly high standards. This has resonance with the diet of denigration and messages of uselessness they may have heard in their family of origin. Poor self-worth, hopelessness and depression may be constant companions for these children. It is important that such tendencies meet counteraction by teachers, and that children are helped to accept that, especially as getting things wrong is an ordinary part of learning. Moreover, troubled children may be a quiet presence in a classroom, and it is important that their despair and feelings of failure do not go unnoticed. Mobilising additional help in the form of an Education, Health and Care Plan (EHCP)[1] for these children may need proactive pursuit by parents or carers.

---

[1] **An Education, Health and Care Plan (EHCP) is a legal document in England and Wales that is drawn up between the Local Education Authority, Health and Social Care and a child's family, or a young person between 16–25. The EHCP identifies a child or young person's needs and sets out additional support to meet those needs and the outcomes desired**

Some children will have developed pseudo self-reliance to avoid feelings of vulnerability and fear originating from a former undependable, neglectful situation where their needs were met only haphazardly. Therefore, dependence on a teacher, or recognising that the teacher may have something of value to teach them, is rather problematic and does not fit with the child's ambition for full control over their own life. Five-year-old Simon, who had endured marked neglect in his first three years, grandiosely told his foster carer that he could teach himself. He had taught himself how to read and write via the internet, he asserted, and a self-authored curriculum that he would research on the web was his preferred mode of education, so he did not need to bother with schools and teachers. This was a claim from a little boy who barely knew the alphabet, but his foster carer appreciated it was a sign of how anxious he was about school. He had behaved similarly when he had first come to live with her, shunning her efforts to take care of him and wanting to entirely look after himself in a rather unrealistic way. Allowing himself to be a child who was cared for took some time, and resorting to a "know it all" position was always a temptation for him at times of stress and new challenges.

Too unsettled to learn

Canham (2006) describes the "failure of latency", when children's development does not reach the relatively calm period usually expected during the years of primary school. In such cases, listening and paying attention in class, absorbing knowledge, doing homework, making friends and participating in group activities, all the things normally linked with primary school education, are impeded. A background history of family breakdown, emotional,

---

within a clear time framework. It was formerly known as a "statement of special educational need". In Scotland, children can be assessed as having "additional support needs" (ASN) (all looked after children are initially assumed to have ASN), and possible support will then be developed within the school.

physical and sexual abuse and trauma continues to intrude on all aspects of the child's functioning because their mind has been overwhelmed by adverse experiences that they are poorly equipped to process. They are rarely at ease. They are unable to regulate their feelings and behaviour. Remnants of the past are easily evoked and ricochet around in their minds. They are often in states of hyper-arousal, hyper-vigilant, restless and fidgety, prone to outbursts of anger and behavioural disturbance that they cannot control. Such children are very noticeable in a classroom as their behaviour is so disruptive, and concentration and learning are so difficult for them. Their restlessness and inattention may lead them to be diagnosed with ADHD.

CASE STUDY

Nine-year-old Robert had been physically abused by both his birth parents and had led a nomadic life of dislocation in various areas of the UK before he was accommodated with foster carers at the age of six. At school he struggled to sit still, he was unable to concentrate on work for long, and academically he was falling behind the rest of his class. He was often non-compliant with his teacher's requests and could be very defiant and challenging in his behaviour. He was also challenging towards his foster carers and pushed against the limits they set. There was particular concern about Robert's bossiness and bullying behaviour towards younger children. Children like Robert who are the victims of violence and abuse can unconsciously step into the shoes of the perpetrator. This turning of the tables, with a smaller child as a frightened and powerless victim, is a way of revealing what has formerly happened to them. It can be hard to feel sympathetic towards children like Robert who are aggressive and disruptive, and to see

> their behaviour as a defensive way of managing their own former history of abuse. However, underneath their noisy disruption, they are struggling to manage deep-seated anxieties and to process unmanageable experiences.

Relationship between school and home

Foster carers and adopters can often receive school reports of problematic incidents, and you may feel criticised and even blamed for your child's behaviour, which can be an unfair emotional burden on top of the resources it takes to look after a child like Robert. When children have a history of trauma, it is not uncommon for blame and criticism to surface in relationships between school and home or indeed in wider network meetings. Blame can be misplaced, for example, when a child is seemingly managing at school, although highly challenging and behaviorally disruptive at home. Equally, schools can come in for high levels of criticism for not doing enough when a child is academically failing. The reality is that the fault actually lies with the perpetrator of the original abuse or neglect, although even then, birth parents rarely consciously intend to harm their children. When misplaced blame is an obstacle to collaborative communication, it may be useful to reflect on whether aspects of the child's birth family situation might be being re-enacted in the present.

Getting additional help

While it is important that school is a protected environment where all children feel safe, behaviorally disturbed children need their place in school too, especially given the severe disadvantages they have experienced in earlier life. Education and Health Care Plans or similar arrangements, incorporating tailored individual educational help and supervised structured time to link with their peers, are beneficial for children like Robert.

Children with entrenched problems that compromise their academic attainment and impact on their emotional and social development may also need CAMHS (Child and Adolescent Mental Health Services) involvement. Individual psychotherapy may be helpful for some children. It is of paramount importance to have a joined-up approach between all the adults: the adopter or foster carer, the social worker, the teacher, and the CAMHS clinician. By sharing experiences and thinking together from their various positions of individual expertise, children can be helped to feel firmly held by a collaborative network.

CHAPTER **5**

Difficulties in learning in adolescence

Turbulent adolescence is an exciting time for young people, playing with ideas and ideologies, questioning assumptions, and working out individual values and beliefs, often in the context of a friendship group that has an absorbing importance. There can be tensions between the academic demands of secondary school, the pull of group life and reaching for one's own individual place in the world.

Transfer to secondary school

Like all transitions, the move into secondary school can revive memories of former key points of change, and for many adopted and fostered children, this will include painful memories of leaving families of origin, changes of foster placements and schools, or social workers leaving and being replaced. The new start at secondary school may feel particularly intense for these children, as it is likely to coincide with all the physical transformation that puberty entails. The emergence of an adult-like body for young people who have experienced trauma, neglect or abuse may bring additional conflicts. For example, if your child was exposed to sexual violence in their early years, even though there may have been many more years in a stable foster home, the awakening of ordinary sexual feelings can feel more complicated.

CASE STUDIES

Fourteen-year-old Louise, for example, was troubled by memories of being sexually abused by her father, whom she hadn't seen for many years, when she became physically intimate with her first boyfriend. Flashbacks of the kind associated with PTSD (Post-Traumatic Stress Disorder) were triggered by her first sexual explorations. She also found attending sex and relationship education at school very problematic, as this again triggered unwelcome memories. Her Head of Year made special arrangements to support her.

Fifteen-year-old Ben was hugely uncomfortable with his newly emerging, strong, powerful physique, which reminded him of his father, who had been violent to both his mother and himself when he was a young child. He had a strong conscious desire not to grow up to be like his father. He was frightened by his own feelings of anger and rebelliousness, never openly expressed, and had begun to attack his own body by self-harming. While he was mild-mannered and placatory in his external relationships at school and keen to de-escalate any signs of conflict, he perceived himself to be intensely angry. He was worried about the harm he could do. He found it increasingly

> difficult to be around people and was withdrawn in class. He could not concentrate and was falling behind with coursework.

Both Louise and Ben were supported by their foster carers and social workers to seek therapeutic help to untangle some of their past traumatic relationships that were now presenting them with acute conflicts to resolve.

Anxiety associated with exams

The academic demands of secondary education are high. Educational progression, competence in coursework and performance in exams can cause anxiety, especially in the context of a competitive group of friends. Some anxiety can be a mobilising force that can help young people to finish assignments. However, anxiety can spiral out of control and become paralysing, so that learning is really hindered. Panic makes it impossible to take anything in, to concentrate.

Young people who are not living with their families of origin may face additional internal pressures. Failure may be unconsciously felt as inevitable, confirming underlying feelings of inadequacy and poor self-regard, qualities imported from former situations. This undertow may be difficult to overcome. Paradoxically, educational success may also feel complicated. Despite academic achievement being connected with satisfaction, it may also mark a direction in life that is very different from that of children's birth families, who may not have been academically successful, valued academic achievement or had challenging and satisfying jobs. This may feel like a betrayal for the young person and lead to feelings of guilt or triumph, and worries about authenticity in claiming success so far removed from the legacy of one's origins.

Belonging to two families

Young people who are fostered or adopted will always have two families in mind, their birth family and the family that chose them. One of the key tasks of adolescence is exploring issues to do with identity, and this may be when young people begin to reflect on their past lives, revisit reasons for not growing up in their birth families, and seek more information to investigate their origins. This can be confusing, emotionally demanding and can divert energy away from formal education, but it is valuable experiential learning for life. It is a chance to construct a more complete life narrative and gain a more integrated sense of self.

CASE STUDY

Sixteen-year-old Eva spent the majority of her life in a stable adoptive home and had intermittent contact with her white English birth mother, who had serious mental health problems. She had met her black Nigerian birth father only once, and while there wasn't a disavowal of her black heritage, it had not featured sufficiently in her life. The prominence of the Black Lives Matter campaign in 2020 prompted her to reappraise her ethnic identity. She went through a period of researching the Nigerian side of her family, and supported by her adopters, tried to trace her father, although without success. She read widely about slavery and African history. This was an intensely preoccupying investigation for her, consuming her passionately for a time, but ultimately it was learning that

> was very helpful in giving her a rounder understanding of who she was and a more consolidated identity as a black young woman.

Eva was engaged in a process of learning about herself in a deeply personal way that was emotionally demanding. At the same time, she was managing the rigours of formal learning in her secondary school, steadied by supportive adopters, and progressing reasonably well. This is not the case for many young people. Sometimes the lure of an abusive past life can unleash self-destructiveness during adolescence that feels impossible to resist, leaving no space for ordinary school demands. Some young people may be beset by feelings of depression and despair, a sense of worthlessness and self-loathing that leads them to question their very existence. Their minds are then not available for education.

Risks posing obstacles to learning

Young people may act very punitively towards their changing bodies in adolescence, and feel ill at ease with approaching adulthood. The emergence of an eating disorder, disciplined starvation in a highly controlled way, or compulsive binge eating may be a maladaptive way of gaining control over physical changes. The young person may have significant ambivalence about growing up. Overdoses of medication may be used to quell unbearable emotional pain. Self-harm may be tempting as the preferable experience of physical pain giving relief from emotional suffering.

> **CASE STUDY**
>
> Fourteen-year-old Malachy, who was severely depressed, self-harmed by cutting himself, as the only way he knew to feel momentarily alive. He had lost all interest in school and was only intermittently attending classes.

Recklessness can be associated with ordinary adolescence: staying out all night in risky circumstances, sexual promiscuity and sexual experiences without contraception, experimentation with drugs and excessive drinking. However, when taken to extremes, and habitually and addictively pursued to obliterate feeling, and when there is an absence or disregard for any internal authority that may be self-protective, then it is particularly concerning. Keeping up with coursework and attending school become irrelevancies in these circumstances.

Destructiveness may also, of course, be a group activity. There may be a strong pull to join a gang which, ostensibly at least, offers a place of belonging at just the point in life when self-doubt and rootlessness are most strongly felt. There is a broad spectrum of gang activity ranging from peer group gangs in schools or in localities, engaged in scapegoating and bullying, racist gangs, to gangs that commit minor street crime and get into trouble with the police. Bullying and intimidating other people ensures that fear is felt elsewhere, while providing a pseudo-secure base for gang members, with all vulnerability kept at bay. On the more extreme end of the continuum are powerful organised criminal gangs that proactively recruit vulnerable young people, often online, and manipulate them with false promises of better alternative lives that exploit their emotional weaknesses. Gangs are essentially anti-development and anti-learning. When young people are taken over by gang activity, their availability for formal learning at school suffers.

The re-negotiation of identity in adolescence involves coming to terms with loss – the loss of childhood, and for fostered and adopted children, the loss of the birth family and perhaps the loss of the idealised family they craved from birth. It is a painful process of upheaval and conflict that can challenge both home and school. Sometimes, the most dedicated and caring of foster carers and adopters may not be able to withstand the extent of disturbance and challenges. Unfortunately, this can be a time when placements become vulnerable to disruption. Similarly, school staff may not feel able to support young people through elongated stormy periods when they are disengaged from learning and loudly impacting on classroom functioning, and sadly, some young people will be excluded from school. However, it is important to bear in mind that the revisiting of past trauma during adolescence and the exploration of former experiences do not necessarily lead to disaster. Many young people are resilient and reflective and their education does not terminally go off course. There is a reckoning with the past that can facilitate development. With the right support, young people can continue to learn, in order to move towards adulthood with more capacity for independence and with more internal solidity to face new challenges ahead.

CHAPTER 6

How to help

Foster carers and adopters are unlikely to accompany their children and young people on their educational journey without some challenges along the way. This is to be expected, whatever the circumstances. However, when children's early years are characterised by unreliable care, an unusually high level of change and disruption, and/or traumatic experience, the educational challenges may be greater.

Learning is never isolated from other aspects of a child's functioning and life circumstances. The previous chapters have shown that helping a child to learn involves nurturing curiosity and creativity by attentive, caring adults in circumstances that feel safe. This can take time and patience to establish. Often, the support provided by a foster or adoptive family will be sufficient to move children and young people onto a more settled pathway so that they are more able to learn and develop. However, some children and young people may continue to struggle and will require additional help.

There are a number of websites and organisations (See 'Useful organisations' later in this book) that are valuable resources for finding advice. In addition, the following are points for general guidance and areas to keep in mind, which may well be relevant for all children and young people, but will have special importance for those who have had difficult beginnings in life and experienced emotional obstacles to learning.

Promote play

When children have not had opportunities to play in early life, their capacity to learn is hampered. They may not know how to play or their play may be very inhibited. Free play is what children do naturally and exuberantly when they grow up in "ordinary" circumstances and it cannot be taught, but any small signs of interest in play or expression of playfulness, however limited, should be encouraged and endorsed. A helpful approach can be for you, as a parent or carer, to establish the routine of having short play periods together with your child each day, and being attentive and interested in any child-led activity. Even the tiniest inclination towards exploration by passive or withdrawn young children is worth noting and developing. Additionally, efforts to involve children in more structured games that include taking turns may spark interest for a short period, and if this can be extended even briefly before they get distracted, it will allow their attention span to grow little by little. Learning requires attention and concentration so this is time well spent.

Notice when children's challenging behaviour occurs and think about its meaning

Disturbed, challenging and disruptive behaviour is a form of communication for children that precedes access to any insight or verbal communication about what might be the matter. A child may trash a room because of the urgency to discharge an overwhelming feeling, without any clear sense of the source of their disturbance. This lashing out quickly externalises problems and is contrary to what is required in order to learn: taking things in and staying with the emotional discomfort of trying to understand something new. Therefore, putting effort into helping your child to understand the meaning of behavioural outbursts is worthwhile. It introduces a higher-level way of processing experience that engages the mind rather than "letting the body do the talking" through action.

As a foster carer or adopter, you are likely to have observed your child's pattern of distress and challenging behaviour, and to have some knowledge of its origins, however incomplete. While it is never really possible to have a discussion with a child in the midst of a behavioural storm, and the focus at this time has to be on physical safety, when things calm down it becomes more possible to talk with your child and review what happened. It is helpful to make the connection for your child between the possible trigger and the outburst, because children are unlikely to have any idea of why they became so distressed. This can be done in quite simple ways. For example, if there is always a major outburst when a child cannot immediately find something that is missing, this observation can be shared later. Speculative wondering about the underlying reasons gives a sense of meaning to the behaviour. Putting it into words introduces verbal expression as a way of processing the experience. Thinking and cognitive processing, central to learning, are thus introduced as an alternative to behavioural release of upset.

With repetition of this retrospective processing over time, there is the possibility of slow gradual internalisation, so that your child is able to think about behaviour and the meaning it has. When the identifying and naming of difficulties become more possible, behavioural eruption may gradually decline or become less intense. This facilitates more availability for learning.

Prepare in advance for any known change or transition

It is a normal experience to have some internal resistance to change, as accommodating any new experience involves some level of anxiety about the unknown (Salzberger-Wittenberg, 2013). This has implications for learning, which is a process that has grappling with uncertainty and the unknown at its core. Children who are fostered or adopted have possibly had numerous changes with which to contend, often including a number of different placements before adoption, changes of social workers and changes of schools. Additionally, changes may have happened in a rather sudden, unplanned way. Any change or transition therefore is likely to be particularly disturbing for those children who have had serial significant changes in their background. A new transition may trigger a sense of loss and a range of memories and associated feelings about former losses, including removal from their families of origin. High levels of anxiety are likely to be mobilised at points of transition, which interferes with the child's openness to new experience and learning. It is not possible to learn when overwhelmed with anxiety.

Relatively small changes, like a classroom being painted a different colour or the introduction of a new library corner, can be unsettling. A supply teacher replacing your child's usual teacher for a few days may be devastating. Moving from the weekend to Monday morning, returning to school after half-term or longer holiday periods, may become tempestuous. Preparation in advance regarding any known change will usually be beneficial. Discussing with your child anticipated difficulties and problems connected with any change ahead is likely to relieve their anxiety. Space for acknowledging dislike of approaching change, even though it still has to be experienced, at least allows your child to feel understood. These kinds of conversations are likely to bring down children's anxiety levels, and build resilience in relation to change and openness to learning.

Expect setbacks in learning

Learning is never a linear process with progressive development. There are surges forward in understanding followed by setbacks when all improvement seems lost. This can be disheartening, but it simply reflects the nature of learning. Children who have been denigrated and made to feel worthless are prone to give up on learning; they feel it is not worth bothering because they will fail in any case. They need a great deal of encouragement to put effort into learning and to keep on trying. Praise of achievements, and reminders that getting things wrong and making mistakes are an expected part of learning, are helpful for all children. However, fostered and adopted children, who often have poor self-esteem, may need additional encouragement in order to keep them motivated, and reassurance that they are accepted irrespective of their academic attainment.

Make time to talk about difference and diversity

Children and young people in the UK are growing up in a diverse society, and openness to a range of differences – gender, sexual orientation, ethnic, religious, and cultural difference as well as differences around ability – is potentially interesting and enriching. Yet internalised and unconscious prejudices and assumptions are daily obstacles to treating people perceived to be different with respect. Black and minority ethnic children and young people will routinely be subjected to racist abuse, ranging from threats and actual physical assault to name-calling and subtle and not so subtle micro-aggressions. They are also likely to have witnessed their black foster carers and adopters being subjected to some form of direct or indirect racism. Cumulatively, this has a corrosive impact on mental health and well-being. The impact on learning is also detrimental. Concentration is likely to be problematic when energy has to be diverted to emotionally surviving serial racist abuse. It can take a while to refocus. Repetitive denigration can compromise self-esteem, which in turn can adversely affect confidence and motivation to learn.

Adopted and fostered children often have a triple dose of unfairness to contend with: a history of abuse or neglect and a "different" family as well as the injustice of racism, with the latter potentially triggering echoes of the former experience. In a similar way, young people who are questioning their sexual orientation or gender identity can face homophobic or transphobic abuse, which can become intolerable, as they seek to find a way of being in the world that feels true to who they are. Focus on formal learning and educational attainment may become secondary to a child or young person in the midst of more personal learning about identity and place in the world.

Children and young people need regular opportunities to share experiences of racism and other forms of unfair treatment, rather than allowing their anger to turn inward and to fester. This will help minimise disruption of attention and concentration. Additionally, all children need help to consider how they might hurt others who are seen to be "different". Learning about diversity widens perspective on the world and a respectful attitude towards others is an integral aspect of emotionally healthy relationships.

Be aware that children and young people may be acutely conscious of their different living circumstances

Children and young people grow up in a number of different contexts now, with the traditional nuclear family less prominent than in previous times. Single-parent families have become more common and it is not unusual for children and young people to live in re-constituted families with a parent, a step-parent and half-siblings. Some children live with two same-sex parents. Yet, children and young people who are not living with their birth families may be acutely aware of their different situation when compared to that of others at school. It may be beneficial for you to acknowledge this difference if it is causing upset, and to take seriously your child's feelings of being different by virtue of living in a foster or adoptive family. Discussions about diversity of living arrangements and facilitating introductions to children and young people in similar circumstances may diffuse your child's self-conscious feelings of being the only one who is fostered or adopted.

Expect distortions in the way that children and young people process information

Objective appraisal of information and ordinary day-to-day events is required in the process of learning. The capacity to see things from different angles or viewpoints and to use evidence in putting together a logical argument is routine in many subjects learned at school. Children who have experienced trauma often struggle with sound evaluative skills and may be prone to distorting and misinterpreting information. For example, it is not uncommon

for a child to believe that it was something about the kind of
baby they were that was responsible for their birth mother
taking drugs, abusing alcohol or becoming severely depressed.
Although this is obviously not the case, and clearly a baby cannot
be held responsible for their parents' difficulties, the tendency to
misrepresent situations in ways that skew the child's part in the
scenario, may be an underlying difficulty that crops up regularly.
Not being invited to a birthday party, for instance, may be viewed
as absolute confirmation of being disliked. Other possibilities are
not considered, like the birthday child only inviting those children
who share their table in class. Opening out these situations as they
occur, and offering alternative explanations to your child that seem
obvious to you but that may be eluding them, will enhance learning,
as it gently challenges flawed thinking, widens perspective and
encourages a more balanced and reasoned assessment of situations.

Cope with being unwanted – it is not personal although it may feel like it at the time

Many foster carers and adopters will have experienced being
rejected and unwanted by children and young people who have
good reason not to trust the adult world. Some will have a shell of
self-sufficiency, omniscience and self-reliance, but underneath this
layer are desperately in need of love, care and help with learning.
An ordinary aspect of growing up involves learning from those
who are older and more experienced. When key opportunities for
learning from foster carers and adopters are apparently shunned
or treated with suspicion by a child, it can be very discouraging.
However, efforts to persist in sharing knowledge and understanding
are very much required, despite appearances to the contrary.

Be aware of digital dangers (and benefits), and social media

Children and young people are growing up in a digital age, and going online is an ordinary part of daily life to seek immediate information, to connect with others on social media and for gaming purposes. During the Covid-19 pandemic, digital connection and online learning were of crucial importance and were often the only ways of maintaining some relationships and continuing education. Digital connectivity remains a positive force. However, as a foster carer or adopter, it may be important for you to make space for discussion about some of the dangers. Cyberbullying causes real distress for children and young people; it may feel less personal because it is not face-to-face, but in reality it is equally pernicious and harmful. Victims of bullying can become withdrawn and disengaged from learning, with adverse impact on academic attainment. Investment in creating perfect selfie photos and over-reliance on approval ratings for social media posts may place too much emphasis on surface appearance. This is the antithesis of real learning through engagement in relationships in a more genuine and holistic way.

Pornography is nowadays all too readily accessible online to children and young people, which distorts learning about real-life sexual relationships. Also, online predators masquerading as children's peers actively recruit vulnerable children for purposes of sexual exploitation or criminal gang activity. This is a worrying and not exhaustive list of risks in the online world, which points to the need for educating children in online safety. Some foster carers and adopters regularly monitor their children's internet use, ensure parental controls are operating, and have discussions with children about online activity to ensure that it has not taken over children's lives in a disproportionate way. Whatever the approach, it is important for you to make space to talk with your child about some of the risks associated with online life.

Anticipate problems in learning from experience

Children who have had traumatic histories are unlikely to have had sufficient foundational learning of the kind described in Chapter 2. Repetitive experiences of making connections, and linking cause and effect mediated by adults in early life, will be missing or poorly established. Moreover, ordinary learning from experience is disrupted by the impact of trauma, which makes taking in and retaining information unreliable because of interference from hyper-vigilance, dissociation and disconnection. A new skill can be quickly forgotten in these conditions, and the same mistakes can be made over and over again. On the face of it, this may seem puzzling to an adult. If a child seemingly understands how to put toothpaste on a toothbrush one day after being shown how to do it, why is the lesson lost the next day? This is not willful on the child's behalf, it is because trauma unsettles the ordinary processing of information. Considerable patience is required to show a child the same thing over and over again, to demonstrate connections between cause and effect. With repetition over time, new learning can slowly take root in experience.

Establish a good link with school staff and get help with learning issues

Many fostered or adopted children and young people will have been exposed to adult relationships that have been marked by excessive conflict and argument. By forming a friendly connection with your child's school, you will give your child what may be a new experience of adults collaborating around them, which is likely to be welcome. When teachers and support staff at school are made aware of children's difficulties, they are likely to consider extra help for those who are not progressing with standard classroom support. Although resources across individual schools will vary, it is worth finding out, for instance, whether there are any small groups at your child's school for children who need additional literacy and numeracy support. There may possibly be individual help from a teaching assistant or learning mentor for children lagging behind their peers in key aspects of learning. For those children and young people who are struggling with friendship, relationship or emotional problems, school counselling may be available. It is worth finding out what individual schools offer. If children and young people are not making expected progress with additional learning support at school, and academic attainment is a continuing problem, the next step is to discuss an assessment for an Education and Health Care Plan in England or Wales/Additional Support Needs in Scotland (see previous footnote). While it is possible to apply directly to local authorities for this assessment, it is always best to get agreement from your child's school first and to work co-operatively with them.

Get professional help if emotional and mental health difficulties persist

When difficulties do not resolve after a child moves out of adverse circumstances, and problems persist despite support from school staff, GPs and social workers, further help may be required. However, in some instances, children and young people may need to feel settled for a long period before they can trust those looking after them with some of their deep-seated worries and difficulties. Sometimes problems emerge that are triggered by particular events even after fostered or adopted children seem settled and contented.

When there are marked changes in the way a child or young person is functioning in day-to-day life, for instance, persistent changes in eating habits resulting in weight change, perception of being fat despite evidence to the contrary and going on strict

How to help

diets; deterioration in mood and feeling that life is not worth living or self-harming; flashbacks and intrusive memories associated with former trauma; unusual perceptual experiences, like hearing and seeing things that others do not perceive, then it is important to seek urgent professional advice. GPs can discuss these concerns with you and refer you and your child to Child and Adolescent Mental Health Services (CAMHS) if appropriate. In extreme situations of mental health crisis, if a young person is in immediate danger of suicide and it is not possible to guarantee their safety, an assessment at A&E may be necessary.

However, it is also important not to underestimate the value of a child or young person unburdening themselves by talking with someone close to them. Ensuring that a child or young person knows that you are available is hugely beneficial.

Conclusion

Children and young people who have endured neglect, abuse and traumatic experience in early life are likely to be significantly disadvantaged in their learning capacities. They are likely to lag behind their peers in their absorbing, concentrating, communicating and processing functions because they have not enjoyed the early life experiences necessary to develop in an ordinary, optimal way. Neurological development is impeded by a lack of early loving relationships and insufficient lively, attuned interaction. Protective barriers that have developed in the child's mind in order to screen out unmanageable anxiety connected with neglect, hostility, intrusion and threat, interfere both with learning and allowing relationships that foster development. These defensive barriers are not within children's conscious control and cannot be dismantled easily, at will, when circumstances change.

On the face of it, this seems like rather a bleak outlook for learning. However, many children and young people who have backgrounds of exceptionally adverse experiences show tremendous resilience and hopefulness. Their trust in the adult world can be established or renewed, with effort over time, by caring, thoughtful adults who have their best interests at heart and in mind. Foster carers and adopters who have the day-to-day experience of looking after traumatised children and young people are best placed to know that trust is hard won and precarious, but that endurance does succeed in slowly bringing creativity and playfulness to life and thus engendering the wish to relate, and to learn. Security and consistent care at home usher in the gradual possibility of curiosity and discovery. With the right conditions in place, it is never too late to learn and to develop.

SECTION II

PARENTING CHILDREN AFFECTED BY DIFFICULTIES IN LEARNING CAUSED BY TRAUMA

Our educational journey

Kathleen Grace

Before setting off

At the time I went through the adoption process, I was an experienced primary school teacher, working with children who had a wide range of difficulties and special educational needs. I felt that I knew the education system inside out – from school admission criteria through to leading annual reviews for children with special educational needs – and naively thought, 'At least that's one area I am confident will go smoothly when I adopt'. Somewhere along our journey, I realised that it wasn't my knowledge of the education system that was important, but my knowledge and my understanding of my children.

I heard about two little boys, Shane and Ricky, then aged four and five, who had experienced a very rough ride in life so far – with many moves compounding their high level of trauma. I had been given some out-of-date reports, met their family-finder, and was due to meet their current foster carers. I wanted as much information as possible; my heart was trying to race away with me (and the boys), but my head was staying focused on finding out as much as I could about their history, their lives now, their personalities, their successes, and their difficulties, to help me make an informed decision about becoming their single parent.

Our educational journey started the day I met staff at the school Shane and Ricky were attending. I had eagerly accepted the offer of a visit whilst in the area to meet the boys' foster carers for the first time. I was able to temper my nerves about the whole day by focusing on the afternoon visit to the school, where I expected to feel more relaxed. Ricky and Shane both had full-time support allocated to them through Educational Statements that had been in place since they were in pre-school. They were currently in the same reception and Year 1 class of mixed age groups in the small school that they were attending. I met with the Headteacher, SENCO (Special Educational Needs Co-ordinator), class teacher, pre-school leader (attached to the school), and their current LSAs (Learning Support Assistants); I was privileged to have so much time given to me. However, it didn't turn out to be quite as relaxing as I had imagined. I heard about two boys for whom school life currently appeared to be more about containment than education. Ricky was described as "prowling" around the edge of the classroom, not engaging with any tasks. Shane was said to be willing to sit in a small group but did not appear to have relationships with any adult or peer. The boys ignored each other in class unless one became hyper, at which point they would both run around the school shouting, screaming and knocking everything in their path flying. At the end of our meeting, the staff wished me well, saying they were sure, 'Once the boys are settled in a loving home, their behaviours will improve no end' and, 'All they really need is love'. If only I had realised then just how little most educators knew or understood about attachment and trauma. At that time, I was blinkered; coming from a school where all staff had training in basic child development, had an understanding of attachment theory and how trauma affected both, I assumed other schools did too – and that the staff's words to me were rooted in optimism.

On the long drive home that day, I reflected on the parts of the story I had heard from the boy's foster carers, the respite carers, the school staff, the boys' social worker and their family-finder. By now, I had received some of the many documents I had requested from children's services (many others took several months longer to arrive), but there was a growing sense in me that something was missing. I sat with a friend that evening and, in best teacher style, we organised the jigsaw pieces we had so far. We set out a timeline of Shane and Ricky's life to give coherence to their story, and we peppered that with questions and links between known facts. The impact on me was significant; it felt as if this was the first time anyone had looked at the whole picture, the first time anyone had seen all the broken stepping-stones in the children's lives so far. That night was when I made my decision; I committed to my boys.

The short time after the matching panel was a whirlwind as I prepared – although nothing compared to the rollercoaster ride of that 10 days when the boys and I first met. In that strange goldfish bowl that is "introductions", I saw Ricky and Shane's panic and confusion, their fears of what was happening to them this time, with this move. They didn't understand the concept of adoption and, given their history, they had no expectations of permanence. As I drove home each evening, my thoughts were an echo of Shane and Ricky's fears and panic; I had begun to realise the enormity of the change for us all.

Linking, matching and introductions happened in a fairly short space of time, which meant when my boys finally came home, they didn't have school places. Shane and Ricky had been in foster care in a different local authority to my own and therefore needed not only to change schools but also to have their Statements rewritten. This all took time. Lots of time.

Meanwhile, I visited local schools armed with what little I knew about the boys – but comforted by the fact that I "knew" about schools. I rejected our own "Outstanding" village school without even taking a tour of the building when the then Headteacher welcomed me into his office with the words, 'Oooh, looked after and Statemented, they'll bring in lots of money'. I focused my search on small schools because I'd learned how difficult both boys found crowds of people, loud noises and lots of adults. I also rejected open-plan schools in favour of those with four solid walls around each classroom – remembering the need for containment that their previous school had talked about. I researched staff turnover in the schools I visited – knowing the impact a change of teacher can have; I questioned how trauma- and attachment-aware their schools were; I asked for copies of the behaviour policy – looking for how they dealt with both positive and negative behaviours; I did my homework thoroughly.

When I finally settled on a school, I discovered that they only had one of the spaces I needed. Looked after child priority placing for schools bears no weight against infant class sizes or the normal timings for school admissions. I was also busy persuading the local authority to put both boys back a year in recognition of their disrupted education and their lack of readiness to learn.

Setting off

Ricky and Shane came home one sunny spring morning in what thankfully became a glorious early summer of warm, dry days. They were a force of nature and we spent our first months in a state of shock, trying to learn how to live together and getting to know each other. While the social workers worried about lack of education, I was actually quietly pleased with our time to get to know each other. I had two terrified little boys who displayed such differing needs and who were both significantly behind in many areas of their development. They had experienced so much trauma, chaos and change in their lives; they needed time to settle and for me to learn more about them. In many ways, that first six months together was a gift. Looking back now, I think if school places had been available soon after placement, then life would have been far more difficult. Shane and Ricky would have had to try to manage getting to know me, my family and their new environment whilst also coping with a whole range of other adults and children in school. Those first few months were incredibly hard on the boys; everything was new and unknown. Shane had no concept of who I really was in his life and would happily follow strangers towards their cars. Ricky was in equal parts clingy and rejecting; it was impossible to even go to the bathroom without him coming with me and trying to sit on my lap, but at bedtime he would lash out at me and not let me near him.

We started to carve out our own little routines and I worked to create structure and consistency. We had the year mapped out into seasons, with key events such as birthdays; a visual timeline covering the week ahead with one key event per day; and a more detailed, "Yesterday, Today, Tomorrow" chart – all to give them a sense of time and to build understanding that they were here to stay. At this point, learning for the boys was about creating a sense of safety and permanence. A large part of feeling safe involved food – knowing it was there, knowing what meal was coming next and having meals at set times. We had some chaotic moments in our local supermarket, but the regular weekly food shop, each boy armed with their own shopping list, became a favourite time for us all, and through it they learned to try new foods and expand their previously very limited diet; they also learned to sit at the kitchen table and use cutlery. Each of these achievements felt such a success in our early life together.

Alongside feeling safe, there was learning about the natural world. In foster care, Ricky and Shane had been kept busy all day as a way of managing their behaviours, usually in places with lots of stimulation, noise and crowds. They delighted in the tranquility of our quiet village (while shattering it with their own noise). They needed neverending physical activity, but not the trampoline bouncing recommended by their social worker, which only served to over-excite them further – but long walks, paddling in the sea, climbing trees and rolling down hills served us well. The freedom of not being in school allowed us time to bond, and gave Shane and Ricky a chance for their tightly wound, "wired for stress" bodies to relax a little. The fragility of our developing bond was demonstrated by Shane one day asking when they were moving in with my brother. In my attempts for my boys to slowly become familiar with family (involving slightly longer visits each time, and then an occasion when I left them with my brother whilst I had a review meeting with children's services), I had inadvertently given Shane the impression that he was going through another period of introductions. The process of learning to attach to one key person (other than their brother) hadn't even really begun; it was a timely reminder to me of how very confused Ricky and Shane were about so many things in their lives.

There was a lot of unpicking to do. Ricky and Shane's lives had been full of inconsistencies and chaos that had led to many misconceptions and misunderstandings – both in their skewed view of the world and often also in adults' perceptions of them and their needs. The boys gave out very mixed signals. Shane was desperate to keep adults on his side in his attempt to make sure they didn't harm him; he was charming, compliant and would easily snuggle up to a complete stranger. Ricky had a different strategy for maintaining his safety – he gave death stares to anyone who came near and projected an image of being self-reliant by rejecting any offers of help or support. Educating my family and friends about these defence mechanisms became a priority, and I began to realise how complex navigating school life was going to be. I heard on the last day of the summer term that

Ricky and Shane had been allocated places in my chosen school, starting in the new school year in September. Whilst this was by then welcome news, it meant no time to speak with school staff or to plan how best to support the boys.

As this first six months progressed, it became apparent how much Shane and Ricky had missed out on. They had experienced some good early foster care (which gave me hope for their development), but as I finally received all the requested documents from children's services, the gaps became obvious, and some of the more extreme behaviours that were being played out at home evidenced the reality of their shared history and their extensive trauma bond. We had a failed attempt with some attachment-focused therapy, which wasn't able to match the boys' level of need, and were about to start a short series of sessions of life story work with their family-finder. I knew that the boys needed longer term therapy and started to push for it; they were still in shock from the move to me and were far too unsettled to absorb the rather rapid-fire life story work, especially as it unfortunately overlapped with their return to school.

Despite, or perhaps because of, the gaps in their development, there had been an explosion of progress in those months at home. Ricky had learned to accept wearing his glasses – which resulted in significant improvement in his gross motor skills and some with fine motor skills too; he was starting to be able to dress himself. Shane had grown at the speed of bamboo – moving from the 20th centile to the 50th over that first summer. Both boys came home with significantly delayed speech, but this had improved considerably and both could now be generally understood by people who knew them – although not all the language that slowly became clearer at that time was celebrated! There was a sense, towards the end of the summer, that as a family we were making some progress. I had at times managed to find the right balance between separating Shane and Ricky to allow each their own space and their own toys and us all spending time together as a family unit. We played simple board and card games every day in an attempt to develop turn-taking, communication and that ever-necessary sense of structure. We played with Duplo® together, and I can still feel that squeeze of delight when I think of the first time Shane initiated some imaginative play with a pretend ice cream van I had built for him. I also love a photo I took of a rather quizzical looking Ricky (wondering what on earth I was making a fuss about) the morning he laid out a favourite board game for us to play, without any prompting from me. They had begun to engage with me and the wider world around them. Tiny steps, insignificant to others maybe – but to me, a sign that learning of some kind was happening. That summer I also started to learn; I began to understand the inner workings of a Ricky and a Shane; I began to recognise their different personalities and how that affected them as individuals and as siblings, I began to accept them for who they were instead of what I had imagined they would be, and I began to become an advocate, to be their voice.

Getting lost

In the September of that first year, Ricky and Shane restarted school; having been put back a year in recognition of their lost time in education and their developmental delays due to the trauma they had suffered. They were once again in the same class but each had their own support assistant. I had been able to speak to the Headteacher the morning they were due to start and she had reluctantly agreed to a short transition period and also to me staying in school (not in the classroom) for their first few visits. This was important because both boys had a fear of being abandoned and I now knew from records I had finally received that they had experienced at least one foster care move during a school day – dropped off in school by one carer and picked up later by another whom they had never met.

Ricky and Shane worked up from an initial visit of an hour to staying for the whole school day very quickly, and I was reassured by school staff that everything was going well. Being a teacher myself meant that whilst I had concerns over how well Shane and Ricky were coping, I felt secure in the knowledge that they were being well cared for and supported as much as possible. Our life at home, though, turned from "muddling along" to "absolutely awful". Sleep had been an issue from day one, and we were all suffering the effects of sleep deprivation caused by difficulties with settling, wet beds, nightmares and a wake-up time of 4.30am. Getting ready for school in the morning should have been easy with four full hours in hand. Not so. During our first six months, it had become obvious how much both boys struggled with any transition during their day. Not for us the relaxation of going downstairs in pyjamas for breakfast, and maybe a little play before returning upstairs to get dressed. Choosing clothes each morning hadn't gone well for us either, so by September we had a clear routine of clothes being laid on the bathroom windowsill at night in preparation for the next day. Morning routine was a shared story in my bed, washing and dressing – one at a time while the other looked through the story we had just read or played with a toy – followed by heading downstairs for breakfast. We even cleaned our teeth at the kitchen sink straight after breakfast to avoid the need for going back upstairs. Organisation was key to morning survival in our house – especially since neither Shane nor Ricky could manage being in a different part of the house from me, so if I needed to go back upstairs then we all went back upstairs.

On a school day, organisation was not enough. Military planning alongside precision timing proved more useful – but often still not sufficient. I remember once listening as my wonderfully supportive and knowledgeable social worker gave me strategies for how to manage a child exhibiting such varied and chaotic signs of stress. It was sound advice; she knew her stuff. She queried the doubtful expression on my face and asked if I felt I could at least try some of her suggestions. I replied, 'Well, yes…but what do I do with the other one in the meantime?' My two boys went from being "chalk and cheese" to working as one entity in an instant. I could perhaps get Shane to sit at the table with his bowl of cereal in front of him, but whilst doing that, Ricky would shoot off and tip out all the other cereals onto the floor. By the time I then got Ricky to the table, Shane would have thrown his bowl across it, inevitably causing the contents to make a mess on the table, the floor and to run down the wall. While I sat Ricky down, Shane would run off and urinate over the pile of washing waiting by the machine. And so it went on. It was necessary, particularly at times of stress or difficult behaviour, to separate them as much as possible, because they wound each other up to increasing levels of dysregulation. It was also necessary, particularly at times of stress or difficult behaviour, to keep them as close to me as possible – to provide a sense of security and safety, to limit the potential for destruction and to methodically return to working through the morning routine to ensure they did actually have breakfast and did arrive at school with clothes still on. This is a conundrum I have never fully solved.

Looking back now, I often ask myself why I didn't realise earlier that school was causing so many of our problems. During that first September, I think it was partly that sense that "school was the right thing". After all, I had been a teacher for many years, I had confidence in the education system and I knew what lengths I (and my teacher friends and colleagues) went to in order to provide the right support for each individual child. It was also partly that there were so many other things to blame. A week after starting school, Ricky and Shane started life story work with their family-finder. It was poor timing – but necessary because she was leaving for another post. It also quickly became apparent that the autumn period, right through to Christmas, had many significant trauma triggers for my boys. During our first autumn together, the triggers overwhelmed us all. As a family, we suffered extreme levels of violence (self-harm, child-to-child and child-to-parent), alongside many other challenging behaviours, all tangled in with disclosures from Ricky about their past history; he was beginning to feel safe enough with me to trust me with his memories.

I think for Ricky it was beginning to sink in that we were staying together. By the time they restarted school after the Christmas holiday, it was the longest period of being in one place that they'd ever had without at least respite care. Chlidren's services did offer respite care, but I wasn't keen; the boys needed to know adoption was different from foster care, and that going to stay with unknown people for a weekend was part of their past, not their present or future. Instead, children's services provided a support worker three afternoons a week after school, and also agreed to a year of "high-level" therapy.

Based on the level of support we were by now receiving, and the fact that home life was so difficult, staff at the boys' school appeared to decide that all of the boys' problems stemmed from me: 'It must be your parenting, they're fine at school', 'You're just overanxious because you're a first-time mum', and, 'Relax, they just need time to settle' remarks hit home, and my belief in myself as a mum hit an all-time low. School staff were consistently giving me the message that both Shane and Ricky were "fine" in school. Academically, Shane was learning a little; his hyper-vigilance meant that he absorbed what was going on around him and he also had an exceptional memory. He started learning how to read and proved adept with numbers, but was rapidly falling behind his peers as he was pushed past his missing foundations of learning in order to keep up with the class. Ricky was making no academic progress and there were murmurs from school staff about pursuing a diagnosis of dyslexia. It was the complete opposite of what was happening at home – where Ricky was showing some initial signs of bonding with me and was also starting to learn about, and to enjoy, nature and the wider world. He was curious about how and why things in nature happened, and began to be able to see patterns and then to make links between different situations. Shane appeared to make no links in his life. In many ways, each day was like starting afresh for him; there was no tangible sense that he related anything he had learned to any other situation. Whilst I had worked with many children who initially appeared to have no understanding of the relationship between cause and effect, Shane took this to new limits. He displayed such a high level of dissociation that it was rare to see glimpses of the child hidden behind this trauma survival strategy.

We carried on limping through our life together, but even as winter turned to spring again, and we neared a whole year as a family, we were drowning in a sea of dysregulation. By now it was not just school days causing difficulties with normal daily life, such as having breakfast, going out for a walk or playing with toys. Transitions of any kind had to be planned carefully, but even then, in the time it took me to reassure Ricky by the front door that, yes, his shoelaces were both perfectly even and no, nobody would notice him because of them not lying completely flat across his shoes, Shane had run off, opened the washing machine door and urinated on the clean washing inside. I learned a plethora of strategies during that time – including how to cook, serve, eat and wash up an entire meal one-handed (usually using the other to hold a child's hand to keep him calm).

A particular day from this time is imprinted on my memory. We had planned to visit a local country show and were due to meet my dad (the boys by this time adored Grandad) at the showground at 10am. It was an outdoor event with lots of space and many attractions the boys were eagerly looking forward to – multiple food stands, cars and tractors, animal competitions/ shows and plentiful toilets (a necessity for Shane in particular). I had been in previous years so was able to prepare the boys in advance for what would be there; I had even printed for them both the plan of the showground and marked the things I knew each of them would like. They were so excited, and it felt different from the mania that had surrounded Christmas; they were genuinely looking forward to going.

It was to be our first real outing to an event; it was a beautiful late spring day and I felt supremely confident that the necessary preparation and planning were in place for us all to enjoy the day. Oh, how wrong I was. We successfully navigated the morning routine to the point of being at the front door, putting shoes on and ready to leave. It was as I put my hand on the front door handle that it started to go wrong. Firstly, in Ricky's eyes, his trousers were not falling evenly over the top of his shoes (now velcro rather than laces – I was learning!) and this always upset him. We all trekked upstairs to swap his trousers for shorts; this is not as easy as it sounds when you have a child for whom traumatic memories make it difficult to undress, and when this is further complicated by significant sensory issues with how clothes feel on their skin. We made it down to the front door again, only for Shane to cry that he wanted to wear shorts like his brother – he had refused the offer when upstairs. Back upstairs we went. As we once again started to put our shoes on, Shane lost any sense of calm and instead used his shoes as surface-to-air missiles. If his target was Ricky's head, then he achieved his mission.

Half an hour later, after applying a cold pack and many hugs, we were ready to try again. And so it continued. The boys ate their packed lunch sitting either side of me on the front doorstep while I cried quietly and tried to stay calm enough myself to work out what was going so wrong. I pulled myself together and reasoned we had made progress – we were after all now outside the house. I'm not sure quite what drove me on that day, but I think it was perhaps my own stubbornness and refusal to give up, combined with a sense that we all needed to see this through together, and to learn that we could overcome the difficulties Shane and Ricky faced when confronted by everyday situations. Finally, with many more hurdles along the way, we arrived at the showground at 3.30pm – half an hour before it was due to finish. I was physically harmed (bite marks, scratches and the beginnings of a black eye were all evident) and emotionally exhausted, as were the boys – I was carrying one under each arm, by the time we finally met my dad. The boys wriggled free and ran to their grandad, who swept them up and proceeded to tell them how delighted he was they had come – with no hint of the five-and-a-half hours he had waited for us. Their ease with him that day showed me that they clearly knew he understood them and accepted them for who they were (a relationship that has continued to this day). That memory sits firmly in both my "worst of days" and "best of days" memory files; yes, it was hellish – but we made it.

It became a pivotal day for me. As I reflected back on it that evening, churning through my planning and preparation, the boys' obvious desire to attend the show and everything that had gone wrong, I realised that all my thoughts led me back to the old adage, 'A child uses their behaviour to communicate what they cannot express verbally'. They were clearly telling me that they were stressed, anxious and unable to cope even with things they desperately wanted to do (and that had been adapted for their needs as much as possible). I had been feeling uncomfortable for a while that their teachers were repeatedly telling me there were no issues, that both Shane and Ricky were well settled and everything was "fine" at school (a word I was by then beginning to dread hearing – but heard frequently). I knew I needed to question more and find out what was really happening at school. How could it be possible for Ricky and Shane to be wetting, soiling, dissociating, re-enacting trauma and regressing at home – but show none of this at school? I knew from both training and from experience that many children contain their stress during a school day and explode once in the safety of their own home – but I also knew from experience that the signs were usually there if you made the effort and took the time to look closely. As a teacher, I had witnessed children with dilated pupils, clammy hands and flushed faces. I had smelled the sourness of fear on their breath, counted the endless toilet visits and seen the startled reaction to an unexpected noise or someone getting too close. I also knew, though, that as a profession, teachers are trained to be positive, to focus on what a child can do rather than their difficulties, to praise good behaviour and effort – and sadly, by the time I left teaching, to march steadily forward with targets for academic progress.

After meeting with the boys' class teacher and support staff, I asked the Headteacher if I could lead a whole school staff meeting to give information about Ricky and Shane and their signs of stress. There was resistance to me sharing details of my children in this way; the Headteacher thought it was private information and it became clear that not even the support assistants working one-to-one with my boys had any understanding of their history or their well-documented difficulties. I had moved beyond the point of keeping things private; I needed people around Shane and Ricky to know, not their entire history, but enough of it to see why certain things weren't appropriate, why some routines were vitally important, and what the effects were if those things didn't happen consistently. Most of the staff listened, and I began to hear more open accounts of what had really been happening during the school days – and the accounts were worrying. At my request, a specialist educational psychologist (from our local authority trauma and mental health team) observed the boys in school, gave support and advice to the staff, and wrote the inevitable report – of which I finally received a copy. It confirmed my fears; the school staff were missing many signs of distress, were minimising others, and also mistook (or wanted to see) compliance as a positive behaviour choice rather than as a result of fear.

So many people were fooled by my children's survival strategies – Shane was indiscriminate, everyone loved him, and his smiley defence against actually making any relationship deeper than surface level meant that they couldn't see through to the terrified child. Ricky was viewed as stubborn and controlling – which he was – but most people chose not to think about the reasons why he behaved this way, and many gave up trying to break through his protective shield.

When we met our therapists, it was such a relief to see other people "get it", to have them understand what was going on and where it stemmed from. We were only at the start of our therapy journey, but both Ricky and Shane had completed a thorough series of assessments with our therapy team, which resulted in a comprehensive picture of their diverse and complex needs. From that came therapy and support for us as a family, but also a specialist teacher to see the boys in their school; I felt hopeful that our family could have a good future. What I didn't account for, however, was how entrenched some people are in the views they hold.

"Love is enough", "Time will heal" and "They can't possibly remember, they were too young" attitudes are at best naive and dismissive of the internal pain of childhood trauma, and at worst, truly destructive. Sadly, the school staff were not open to the support the boys were being given, and instead became defensive, blaming behaviours on possible autism spectrum disorder (ASD), attention deficit hyperactivity disorder (ADHD) and dyslexia. To be fair, at the time both Shane and Ricky would have met the criteria for all those diagnoses – and in fact had done so as toddlers in a previous clinical psychologist assessment, which had ultimately diagnosed complex post-traumatic stress and disorganised attachment disorder. There is a lot of crossover between conditions, but I felt strongly that until the boys were showing some signs of feeling a sense of security, there was no point in "labelling" them. Shane, in particular, was definitely going backwards; the regression after school each day was shocking – crawling around on the floor, needing to wear pull-up pants, gagging on food unless it was blended, wailing and babbling like a baby. After yet more attempts to work with the school staff, I made the difficult decision to move them both. In many ways, it felt the wrong thing to do when they had suffered so much change already, but my trust in the school was by now damaged beyond repair.

In the next school, Shane and Ricky were in separate classes and that did help, despite Shane missing Ricky in the classroom. Staff at this school were more willing to take things slowly and we had a prolonged transition, with an ongoing half-day off every week so that each boy could have some individual time with me at home. (Neither had managed full-time school yet, but previously they had had the same day off.) This was valuable time to rebuild the bonds that had started to form during our first six months and that had then been shattered by the stress of school. We were able to return for a while to that sense of "muddling along"; there were still many issues – violence between the boys and towards me being one of the most serious – but therapy was continuing and the sensory strategies before and after school were helping to maintain some semblance of normality. I would meet the boys from school with crunchy and chewy snacks and began to park the car further away in an effort to walk off some of the tension in Ricky's body (thankfully through some quiet footpaths with no traffic). We still rarely made the 15-minute journey home in the car without a few toilet stops for Shane or a meltdown from Ricky. I learned to take the boys' shoes off and put them in the car boot along with their book-bags and water bottles; it was much easier to drive without missiles being launched. I even took to driving somewhere and having a very early meal out, secure in the knowledge that at least then, no matter what happened when we walked through our front door, they had been fed. Whilst the school staff were supportive and listened to most of the advice given by our therapy team, it only took a change of teacher and the boys being in the same class again at the start of the autumn term for things to start going badly wrong. Some staff were unwilling to see the level of need –

especially of needs that were more hidden.

Simple strategies that had worked well in the past, such as being met in the playground by their support staff, were cast aside with a breezy, 'He's in Key Stage 2 now, he doesn't need that any more'. The agreement that support staff would work through elements of homework with the boys as necessary during one-to-one time in school was lost without trace. Poor Ricky arrived home one Friday brandishing a worksheet with 50 times tables questions to be completed by Monday morning. He couldn't consistently read or write numbers one to ten. Fitting in and not being noticed was key for Ricky, so he proceeded to attempt the homework despite all my efforts to persuade him otherwise. It destroyed our entire weekend, and by Monday morning (only two weeks into the new term) I was in the Headteacher's office demanding, with a black eye and swollen nose, to have an urgent meeting with the class teacher. Our children's services support worker (still with us three afternoons a week) came with me to the meeting, and I heard her gasp when the teacher said, 'If I have a bad morning with my husband, I don't bring it into school with me; they just need to learn to leave all their baggage outside my door each day, there's no place for it in the classroom'. The Headteacher did her best, and for a while things improved slightly, but ultimately, education in any real sense was still proving to be unsuccessful.

The impact of the level of stress we were living with meant that, like the proverbial rabbit in the headlights, I was unable to think clearly and followed a course of action rooted in my subconscious (follow advice of professionals – don't question it, children need to be in school/clubs/social activities, I'm a new parent, I know nothing, follow the lead of other parents), rather than following the signs my children were giving me. I still feel guilty about this now. All my years of studying child development, of teaching, of learning about trauma and attachment, and I still couldn't see what was staring me in the face. It took a GP to bring me to my senses. Shane was unable to verbalise his anxieties and his body often took over to show how he felt – through stomach upsets, frequent urination, hives, an inability to control his own body temperature, and with many, many nose bleeds. After a particularly heavy nosebleed at school one day in late September, I took him to see the GP. Her diagnosis? 'His body is not coping with the stress of school.' She wrote a letter for me to say she was recommending a month away from school to allow his body to recuperate. That visit to our GP changed our lives.

Changing direction

I took both boys out of school, initially on a temporary basis. The violence stopped virtually overnight. There were still many issues and difficulties, but the unrelenting violence against me and towards each other became an isolated incident here or there rather than a continuous cycle. Our adoption order had been delayed by my insistence for long-term therapy to be included in our adoption support plan – but that piece of paper now meant that I was no longer dictated to by children's services about the boys having to be in school. The downside was no more visits from my lovely social worker. This was when I began to follow my instincts again and listen to what the boys were telling me by their behaviour. We were once more in that very triggering autumnal part of the year, but this time we were able to shut out many of the external stresses. We returned to the lifestyle of our first six months together; staying near home, keeping mainly to ourselves and finding a structured routine that worked for us.

By the end of October, I had formally de-registered Ricky and Shane from school. Apart from our fortnightly therapy sessions, we were on our own. There was no support from the local authority for home education, and we were left to find our own path; in many ways this suited us, but it also scared me – I didn't know which direction to take. I had read a lot about "unschooling", giving children a time away from all academic learning in order to allow time for them to find their own level, to move away from all the target-setting and assessments. I also knew by now, however, that Shane and Ricky needed structure. The teacher in me niggled away at my conscience; both Ricky and Shane were by now significantly behind their peers in all aspects of learning, surely I should be working hard to help them catch up?

Whilst Shane appeared to show no reaction to suddenly leaving school, Ricky was clearly displeased. It wasn't that he was missing friends; sadly, he didn't have any – mainly due to his lack of social skills, and because he kept his defences high and had no interest in letting even his peers through. He had this need to blend in, to be "normal" and not stand out from the crowd. The effort it took him to try to appear "normal" had been one of the main causes of stress at school. In his mind, not being at school was not normal. Lots of people agreed with him, even me in those early days. I came under criticism about the lack of socialisation and how the boys would never make friends, would miss out on so much…but the reality was, neither boy was making progress socially anyway. They simply couldn't cope. More honest feedback I had been receiving from their second primary school made it clear that Ricky spent playtimes circling round the edge of the playground on his own, watching what was going on but not engaging unless his support assistant led a game with another pupil – and even then, he often wandered off. In class, he wouldn't sit with the other children in a group on the floor, was unable to answer the register or any question in front of others, and didn't participate in any group activity without considerable support.

Shane, on the surface, was the complete opposite. Other children loved playing with him. He was the child who would always run off to collect the football when it had been kicked out of bounds, he was the one who always accepted whatever game the others wanted to play and always took whatever role he was assigned without complaint. Shane gained nothing from it except a spiralling level of dysregulation; within minutes he was sweaty and over-heating (which took hours to subside) and his support assistant would have to withdraw him to play quietly with him away from excess stimulation. In class, the combination of his hyper-vigilance, his dysregulation and his dissociation meant that he spent more time worrying that the teacher had moved a pen on her desk than he did about the given task. His lack of ability to make relationships at any more than surface level had been evident in his inability to recognise staff or pupils in his class if they changed their clothes or styled their hair differently – girls who pulled out their plaits or bunches at playtime and looked different in the next lesson caused him confusion and made him feel unsafe – for him they became unknown people and that brought trauma memories crashing back. Knowing all this, I wasn't worried about the boys missing out socially any more than they already had.

We survived the build-up to Christmas, and once the new year began, we were settled back into a life with no separation from each other. It was difficult; there were no halcyon days of going with the flow and seeing where the day took us. The trauma bond between the boys was complex and provided an ever-present challenge of how to balance their need to feel part of a family unit with the difficulties of their relationship with each other. When they first came home, Shane had been the more dominant of the two; he had appeared more confident and had led their behaviours. Over time, as Ricky began to attach to me and feel more secure, he had become the more dominant, and it was now apparent that Shane desperately needed and wanted Ricky's attention in a way that wasn't reciprocated. This was a massive shift for two boys who had clung to each other physically and emotionally throughout their lives so far.

The emotional upheaval caused by this change in their relationship allowed me to take both of them back to basics. Shane had regressed to infant stage, presenting as a baby with separation anxiety – from his brother. Ricky was much like a toddler, especially in his battles for control. He was at that stage of wanting to explore more of the world. but he was struggling to find a balance between the need to cling to me for safety and his desire to be independent; he wholeheartedly embraced the toddler tantrum stage, but with an eight-year-old's strength and stamina. I was going through my own emotional crisis as I struggled to deal with guilt at having left them unhappy for so long, anger at the advice I had received from some professionals in children's services and education services (who hadn't spent enough time with the boys to understand the extent of trauma my children were dealing with), and doubt over my decision and in my ability to teach my own children.

The return of springtime marked four years of our family tree, and the tight early rings of our life clinging together were enveloped by a wider ring depicting substantial growth. The sense of calm created by a routine and structure based on their individual needs, without social pressure and academic expectation, allowed Shane and Ricky to begin to learn to trust – in both me and the wider world. Whilst the postman walking up to our door still caused unease and revealed their fear of being "taken away" by any adult, both Ricky and Shane were now able to pass people in a shop without flinching. This greater sense of safety enabled them to stop and think before acting (well, sometimes). There was progress with listening to, and understanding, instructions – although Ricky's control issues meant that not many were actually followed! We had, by now, long passed the length of time they had stayed in one place previously; for Ricky this was important, and he became noticeably more settled and willing to talk about "our car", "our village" and "our home".

Shane's separation anxiety and regression demonstrated his need to revisit his early developmental stages – but without the chaos that had surrounded him the first time. He loved being outside exploring nature (and sometimes eating it – I learned to carry a "British flora and fauna" book with me to check if anything he'd just eaten was poisonous) – and he finally began to understand the passage of time through watching the tides and the changes in each season. He was able to recognise the repeating patterns of the natural world and started to relate them to the pattern of our family life. Shane had so little sense of who he was and how he fitted into the world that he didn't feel any pressure to be "normal". He happily displayed his delayed developmental stage for all who took the time to see – a complete contrast to his brother's greater awareness of social norms and resulting inner battle to act his chronological age. I was facing my own societal pressures: it is standard to push for diagnoses when children are not progressing academically or socially, and some people questioned my not doing this. I think I was lucky. I didn't need to follow this route in the way so many parents have to; EHCPs (Educational Health and Care Plans) with accompanying support and therapy were already in place. My opinion was that it remained impossible to know at this point whether either child was showing disordered development due to an underlying condition or delayed development due to their early life experiences and missed foundations. I also worried that by labelling one area of difficulty, it would in some way serve to hide others and therefore obscure the picture of the whole child in favour of focusing support on one aspect, which could have been a further injustice done to Ricky and Shane.

We revisited many of those early life events that help to build the sense of familiarity, continuity and containment that are so vital to healthy development – but this time with embedded structure and routine. Visits to the GP, the hairdresser and the library allowed Shane and Ricky to experience the normality (and, at times, boredom) of everyday life, much in the way a baby or toddler would. The purpose behind much of this was learning to "be" rather than "do"; to try and reduce the hyper-vigilance and to learn to regulate themselves. We also had times of great fun – rolling down grassy hills, picking blackberries and then laughing at purple tongues and fingers, kicking through autumn leaves, and squealing with a mix of pleasure and shock as the tide lapped at our feet. However, sadly, fun times were difficult to manage because the speed and ease with which Shane, especially, tipped into dysregulation was an ever-present challenge to overcome.

In the first year out of school, Shane's stress symptoms became significantly worse and I worried that I had made the wrong choice for him. Our therapists helped me to analyse what was happening and why. They suggested two main possibilities; one being that now Ricky was less violent and no longer constantly acting out, Shane had "space" to show his own feelings. The other was that Shane, for the first time, was feeling safe enough to allow me to see just how traumatised he was and how much that impacted on his daily life. I believe both of these were true; my boys still seem to almost take it in turns to show their distress (Ricky inevitably first, often displaying anxiety before an event; Shane then reacting, usually after an event – once Ricky has settled). Now he was at home with me full time, Shane was relaxed enough to startle at an unexpected noise or to show he was fearful of new people by not talking to them. It somehow seemed back-to-front, but as it had been Shane's defence strategy to be always polite, well behaved and charming, it was in fact progress that he was no longer entrenched in that survival tactic – although he continued to deploy it in public and people therefore failed to recognise his level of need.

We eventually fell into a routine of structured, academic work in the mornings and less formal learning in the afternoons. Although some work – handwriting, spelling, mental maths – was discrete, most of our other academic learning was through lots of play, crafts and other experiential lessons bound together in a topic. We learned about 'The World', 'Invaders and Settlers', 'Animals', and lots more. Only yesterday, my now late-teenage Ricky reminisced about the fun we had on our theme days – the food we cooked as we learned about different countries, the shields we made and mock battles we fought as we pretended to be Vikings and Anglo Saxons. We didn't follow a school-based curriculum, more the interests of my children mixed in with some elements of what they might have been studying were they still in school. I chose areas of learning I knew could include physical activity and places to visit. The wealth of information on the internet was valuable; I often learned only a week or so ahead of my children. Other parents shared their links to online resources and suggested workbooks for particular skills. I didn't use the complete teaching programmes that were available for every subject imaginable, partly because many used "face-to-face" online lessons that my children wouldn't have managed – but also because Ricky and Shane needed to go at their own individual pace. There were many days when academic learning gave way to a more pressing emotional or attachment need. It was vital to be first and foremost their parent, their attachment figure and their point of safety. I naturally gravitated towards being their mum first, despite all my years of teaching.

On my own in the evenings, however, I did mourn the lost education time and worried about what it meant for the boys' futures – but the voices of reason from my sister, my friend and our therapists helped remind me (time and again) that without safety, security and attachment, there would be little other learning. They helped me to recognise that by seeking a solution for our children's difficulties, we can so easily fall into identifying separate issues but lose seeing the whole child. The risk of that is, while there may be progress on the surface, the roots will still be damaged and growth will not be healthy or prolonged. Much as those days of disrupted formal schooling troubled my teacher's instinct, they were a salve to my mothering one – every day helped to dig deeper into the roots of Shane and Ricky's trauma and see the real thoughts, feelings and personalities hidden under all their barriers.

This was in many ways the most settled time of Ricky and Shane's lives. There was an exponential growth in non-academic learning – feeling safe, starting to trust, learning about nature, getting to know family and being able to cope with new surroundings when we went on short trips around the country. As the boys became more settled, we were able to visit museums and had the luxury of doing so when they were not busy; we have a fridge ornamented with magnets, which tell their own story of our educational journey – from the Natural History Museum, through our visit to Battle near Hastings, and on to the National Space Centre.

Greater security led to us joining a few home education groups. Social activities were still too tricky, but those with structure or an academic base were more manageable; Shane and Ricky tended to stay on the fringes, but usually engaged with the subject, and they had the reassurance of me always being in the same room. I admit to being nearly as nervous as my children about joining some of these groups, but our former support worker had put me in touch with another adoptive family (who had chosen home education from the start), and they helped me to work out which groups would be most appropriate. The wealth of different activities and groups was a complete surprise to me; it was almost a hidden education system run entirely by volunteers: everything from cinema and bowling trips through to formal GCSE and A level lessons. The parents and children were from all sorts of backgrounds, from those using it as a way to cram for 11+ or entrance exams, to those who believed in a completely child-led approach without any structure or direct teaching from the adult. There were enough groups, even in our rural area, to choose those that matched with my own developing philosophy – that the safer and happier my children were, the more they would learn. The support I received from these groups was huge. No matter what reasons they had for home educating, or what philosophy they were following, there was an amazing sense of acceptance and understanding from everyone we met. Some of the children had far greater behaviour and learning difficulties than Ricky and Shane, many others were beautifully behaved, and a few displayed exceptional academic ability – but put them all on a gymnastics mat and they supported and encouraged each other without adult intervention. For the first time in his life, Ricky began to feel accepted and the impact on his confidence was profound; he started to be able to play and work alongside other children. He began to make friends. He was now secure enough with a primary attachment to me, to begin to risk secondary attachments to others. I'm not sure if this acceptance was felt by Shane; in many ways he is so much more complex than his brother and interpreting his behaviour is trickier. There was a change in him too, however: he started to expect me to be there for him. There was by no means the depth of attachment Ricky was displaying, but Shane did now know that I was the one who would tend to his injuries and provide comfort and a sense of safety when he was struggling.

On a purely academic level, there was also progress. Soon after leaving school, aged eight, Ricky had finally learned to read. It became evident that dyslexia was not what had been holding him back, although his poor short-term memory was definitely a factor. He quickly grew to love reading (I would like to claim all my hours of reading to my boys led to this – and plenty of studies would support that theory), and even now, eight years later, he reads for at least an hour a day. But despite progress, Shane and Ricky were simply unable to work at the pace of other children of their age, and the gap widened considerably. Teasing out the impact of my children's many years of trauma will be a life-long study and involve therapy with professionals far more knowledgeable than me – but I knew enough about child development and teaching to make a start. Shane, in particular, presented with a very spiky profile – huge strengths in some areas (physical skills and memory-based learning) contrasted by considerable weaknesses in others (reading with comprehension and applying knowledge in everyday situations). Both needed a holistic approach based on their stage not their age; even Ricky was finally beginning to relax without social pressure to conform, and accept the need to "learn to walk before he could run". I was able to see that, apart from a few specific issues, both Ricky and Shane were making progress at their own rate and in different areas in the manner appropriate to their developmental stage; they were showing classic signs of "delayed learning" rather than "disordered learning". Without all their adverse experiences, it is likely that they could have made academic progress at a similar rate to their peers. Whilst this was in many ways a positive realisation, I felt sadness and anger that, through no fault of their own, they would most likely always be behind their peers. Nowadays, with vocational courses and a plethora of adult learning programmes, education is accessible throughout life – which is something I cling to when I worry about my children's future; but that doesn't take away the reality that Shane and Ricky have been denied a normal pathway through life, and I can empathise with the frustration and anger my children have bubbling inside.

Therapy has helped all of us to manage some of these feelings, but as the boys hit different developmental milestones, there are always new challenges to face and they have to work hard to overcome them. "Barriers to learning" is a phrase used most often in reference to specific conditions or global delay, but I feel it is more relevant to the social and emotional effects of trauma. The barriers for my children are not that they "cannot" learn a particular skill or need a specific style of teaching, it is more that low self-esteem, fear of change, extreme feelings of shame, the need to control, and the inability to manage transitions all pile on top of each other to create a seemingly impenetrable wall.

What was becoming more obvious was how, despite the purely academic gap widening, many people were commenting on Ricky and Shane's general knowledge of historical events, scientific processes, the natural world

— and their increasing social skills and emotional stability. Their wider learning of the world as a whole, unconfined by a school curriculum, was starting to show. Shane became interested in planes (mainly military ones) and learned about the history that led to their creation, the geography of certain places that led to different designs and uses, the science of flying and the testing… he knows far more about the World Wars than I have taught him. Ricky is a natural engineer and his love of cars drove him to explore not only the related maths, science and technology, but also the creative minds and artistic talents of those who create the initial vision. I am so proud of both of them; beneath all their difficulties, they share a natural love of learning. But the reality was that to catch up with their peers before the end of their "school" years, they would need to far surpass the pace at which their peers were progressing. That wasn't going to happen. We still had many days when surviving through to bedtime was our only achievement. The motto, "You learn something new every day", which my own Year 6 primary school teacher had drummed into me, was still true — whether that learning was a historically significant date, learning to spell a tricky word or learning that a difficult day was always ended with a hug and the promise of a fresh start the next day.

Acceptance within the home education groups and his developing coping skills led Ricky to join a mainstream sports club, which he loved. Whilst he, by now, openly admitted that he didn't enjoy group activities, especially less structured ones, he allowed me to persuade him into trying — perhaps induced by the fact it was an individual sport, albeit with group training. I'm not sure if by chance I happened upon a particularly supportive and understanding club — but he was understood, accepted and, for the first time, he thrived in a public arena. In advance of his first competition, the club acted thoughtfully and made provisions for me to accompany him at all stages of the event. I had prepared strategies (mainly involving lots of snacks), and had techniques planned to help him through. It wasn't easy for him, but he did it. My pride in his participation was immense; it was such an achievement for him. This feeling, however, was quickly overshadowed – by his request to tell my sister. He was finally willing to feel some pride of his own. That was a far more significant step than competing in a sports event, and I wept unashamedly as I made the call (to the softly voiced mock horror of Ricky's 'Oh, Mummy!').

Shane was a natural at many sports, but struggled with the noise in a group, the pace of instructions, the transitions and changes of tempo, and the expectations to be social. Through trial and error, we found a sport that he could start as an individual and then later join small groups as and when he was ready. With so little time apart from each other, creating a sense of space and independence in sport was important. Shane's distress at being apart from Ricky for any length of time made it hard for him to focus even on a sport he was growing to love. He needed the security of his brother beside him, but if Ricky joined him, Shane would often perform badly – perhaps a subconscious strategy to let Ricky "win" and therefore please him, or a more deliberate ploy to show his subservience to a brother from whom he desperately craved attention and affection. It was a very unhealthy aspect of their relationship, and helped neither of them.

By this time, there was a growing gulf between the

boys' needs; Shane was still a lost little boy struggling to come to terms with all aspects of his life. In therapy, he showed little understanding of his past and how it had shaped his behaviours. He fought daily to maintain his perception of being a major part of Ricky's life – when the reality was that he always would be, but Ricky was moving away from the old patterns that had bound them to each other. Shane couldn't plan ahead to see a future for himself – he frequently used our family memories to ground and reassure himself, but he was unable to move beyond them – for instance, to plan our next trips together. He was stuck. In contrast, Ricky was proving that he now had an ability to find ways to manage his anxieties and the stresses daily life outside our family bubble caused him. It was time to change paths.

Separate paths

When Ricky was 10, I started to plan ahead for a return to school. He wasn't quite ready but was heading in that direction, and I took time to research the options available in the hope that he could rejoin for the last year in primary school. Our local secondary schools are all exceptionally large and that was enough to know that they wouldn't be suitable for him. Instead, I chose an SEN (Special Educational Needs) school with small classes and a good understanding of hidden difficulties – which I felt would meet Ricky's needs well. The local authority disagreed. They wanted to place him in one-to-one provision, but I knew he needed a small group environment. They then suggested a school 45 miles away in another county, then a pupil referral unit 40 miles in the other direction, and on it went. In order to return to school, Ricky's EHCP needed updating and the local authority's part of the paperwork was subject to delay after delay. When the draft copy eventually arrived, the child it described bore no resemblance to Ricky or his needs.

It became a farce. The placement panel decided that Ricky's needs were too great for the small, specialist school I had chosen – so the local authority offered him a place at a mainstream secondary (in another district) with over 1,500 pupils. After two years of relentless pushing, and faced with further delays and refusals to accept the true level of Ricky's needs, I had to employ a solicitor. The local authority finally agreed to the placement I had initially asked for, but sadly the battle wasn't fully over, and although Ricky started at the school with a gradual transition when he was 12, it took another year, and an EHCP tribunal, before the specified provision fully reflected his needs.

Running parallel to the stress, time and paperwork of managing this fight was the stark reality that I had chosen to separate Shane and Ricky – and they didn't yet know. It had been a very difficult decision to make, but Shane just wasn't ready. He needed time to come out from under his brother's influence and learn to be himself. He needed the time and space to attach to me rather than only to Ricky. I didn't want to damage the brothers' relationship, but Shane's desperation to cling to old patterns was stopping him from progressing emotionally – and Ricky needed to learn that he didn't have to be responsible for his brother. It was a tough period for all of us. Shane grieved for his brother and shunned me every day for the first four months. He sabotaged our morning routine in ever more creative and disturbing ways in the hope of preventing Ricky leaving, and then didn't manage to reconnect well after school. I felt a huge sense of guilt over my choice as I watched him struggle; he would accept no comfort or reasoning. It was the right choice for both Shane and Ricky as individuals – but it really didn't feel like it in those first few months!

While his brother pined, Ricky embraced the separation and his chance to have time away from both his brother and me. But the transition was very gradual, and it took 18 months to build up to three full school days. Even then, with only an hour away from me initially, Ricky needed to come home and sit, curled up on my lap, for an hour or more. He used this physical contact to regulate himself and to reconnect; after that phase, he required physical activities to burn off the built-up stress – before eating through a mountain of food and then falling into an often restless sleep. In his special school, Ricky began to accept his own difficulties for the first time, as he saw others needing (and importantly for him, receiving) more help than him. There was a noticeable change in his personality as he began to reflect on others' needs; he became insightful, empathic and (at times) less controlling. Ricky's progress academically was slow but steady, and he demonstrated an ability to generalise his knowledge across contexts. There was an opening of his mind and a raising of the many shutters he used to protect himself (they still automatically come down at times of stress). There were, of course, bumps in the road, but the staff at school were understanding, they listened to, and worked with, our therapists – and most of all, they respected my knowledge of my son. Ricky picked up on this and felt safe there.

Ricky started to make friends and become more confident socially. By the time he was 14, he had been nominated by other members of his sports club for an outstanding achievement award, and had also started to volunteer in our community as part of his Duke of Edinburgh Award.

Shane mourned deeply – but he gradually allowed me to be there with him in that grief. Over time, he started to realise that he could survive without Ricky and began to develop emotionally. He was in many ways still an infant, but there were signs of an emerging personality of his own. He began to recognise hunger, thirst and the feeling of being full. At the age of 12, he woke for the first time to use the toilet in the night rather than wet the bed. We now concentrated far less on academic work and more on emotional development and relationships; he needed the one-on-one time he had never had. Shane had always deferred to Ricky for any decision (no matter how small), but suddenly there were requests for certain meals or for us to go for a walk instead of a swim.

Increasingly, Shane was able to let me into his world and, without his brother to follow, it became clear quite how much he struggled with his understanding of the real world around him. I think the years of dissociation, dysregulation and lack of an adult attachment figure caused him to live his life in little bubbles, in the "here and now", with no overlap. It would certainly explain why he could not link cause and effect, and didn't appear to learn from his mistakes. When we went to watch Ricky at his sports club, Shane would take a flask of hot chocolate. Every single time, over a period of about two years until he stopped taking a hot drink, he would burn his mouth, unable to realise that the drink was still hot. This spilled over into academic learning. Shane had an exceptional memory in some ways (part of his hyper-vigilance), but although he could learn strategies such as long division, he didn't understand what he was doing it for, or when to apply it. Despite this, his self-confidence was growing as he learned that he could do things without his brother. Shane's emotional development, which had been stuck for so long, moved on; in a major step forward, he had begun to initiate hugs with me – fleeting and stiff at first but, over time, he relaxed and seemed to derive comfort from them.

After over a year at home without his brother as a constant companion, Shane, now aged 13, was also starting to show signs of being ready to go back to school. I wasn't as confident as I had been with Ricky that he was ready for friendship or even for being part of a group, but I no longer felt that he would be overwhelmed by school. Additionally, my faith in teachers and the education system had been restored by my experiences with Ricky's school – and I now had the confidence to advocate for my boys until the provision was right. After much consideration, I chose to send Shane to the same school as Ricky; the staff there knew our family history, they had proved adept at understanding and supporting Ricky, and the boys would always be in separate classes. I did worry that Shane returning to school would damage our developing relationship or send him backwards into old survival strategies, but with approaching teenage years, I felt it was "now or never". The route back to school was easier the second time around; I had learned to push for the placement first and finalise the details of the paperwork later (a sensible choice given that nearly two years later we are once again heading to tribunal having only recently received the amended EHCP).

Shane returned to school with a very gradual transition programme, and was starting to integrate into his class while still having plenty of time at home with me. And then…

The sudden return home

Covid-19 struck and so began our second foray into home education; this one not of my choosing. Having Shane and Ricky suddenly thrust back together full time was a challenge as their needs had become more diverse and the effective ways of dealing with them, more individual. The world suddenly became a frightening place again and they both needed reassurance that our little bubble was still safe. They began to be fearful of people again, and this was heartbreaking to watch. I resurrected some old routines and structures to bring back that sense of safety and familiarity in a very uncertain time. Ricky was exceedingly resistant to home schooling again; I was no longer "enough" for Ricky. He is sufficiently secure in our relationship to want to spend time away from me – he missed his friends, sports club and school. Despite regressing to an overwhelming need to control, Ricky was showing some signs of maturity in his outlook on life and what he understood about the world; there was a new ability to assess risk, to reflect, and to let some of his vulnerabilities show.

Once the initial shock wore off and we found our rhythm again, Shane, in particular, seemed to thrive. He had long enjoyed the natural world and was now able to feel a sense of freedom in it – the peace and quiet, the lack of unnecessary contact, the space people gave him. There was remarkable sudden progress in his sleep pattern – at the age of 14, he slept through a whole night for the first time. He started to be truly affectionate and he verbalised his own needs (even when they differed from Ricky's).

The last year, with its rollercoaster of lockdowns, school returns and easing of restrictions seemingly stuck in a loop, has been distressingly difficult at times – and amazingly wonderful at others. Both my boys have been better able to cope with school, coming home less stressed, and I wonder how much of that is the increased structure, enforced distance and lack of movement between classrooms. Shane is more able to identify things that he has found difficult. He is starting to talk about one or two children with greater frequency; although they don't appear to be "friends" yet, I have hope that he now has some of the skills to head that way. Ricky is attending school for three full days again and is coping well. He is in his exam years, has favourite subjects, and tells me about his school day. I know when things haven't gone well for him, but now, given some support and time, he can usually identify and name for himself what has happened.

Each lockdown, we've gone full circle again – but every time that circle has widened and my boys have coped with more. There is the familiarity of having done this before and the reassurance that we'll still be here to do it again. Our family tree has grown, each circle has made our roots deeper, the trunk stronger and the branches able to spread wider. The boys have an increasing sense of awe and wonder at the natural world and an ability to "let themselves go" and be the age they need to be; Shane and Ricky are finally allowing themselves to experience the young childhood they never had. They can only do this in the relative privacy of lockdown;

Ricky, especially, feels the need to hide so much of himself from the wider world – but seeing their joy at watching some foxes rough and tumble together or sensing their relaxation as they laugh at a minor mistake they have made, is so very heartening.

We have taken an unconventional route through the world of education, but Ricky and Shane have taught me to recognise each tiny step forward and to celebrate it. They have demonstrated that underneath all their trauma, and behind all those barriers, they share a natural love of learning. I am immensely proud of all they have achieved after such a traumatic start – but what I love most of all is that they are discovering for themselves that it's OK to be different and to do things differently.

References

Bion WR (1962) *Learning from Experience*, London: Heinemann

Canham H (2006) 'Latency', in Youell B (ed) *The Learning Relationship: Psychoanalytic thinking in education*, London: Karnac Books

Gerhardt S (2004) *Why Love Matters: How affection shapes a baby's brain*, London: Routledge

Rosen M and Oxenbury H (1989) *We're Going on a Bear Hunt*, London: Walker Books

Salzberger-Wittenberg I (2013) *Experiencing Endings and Beginnings*, London: Karnac Books

Sendak M (1963) *Where the Wild Things Are*, New York, NY: Harper and Rowe

Waddell M (2018) *On Adolescence*, Oxford: Routledge

Youell B (2006) *The Learning Relationship: Psychoanalytic thinking in education*, London: Karnac Books

Useful CoramBAAF books

Alix S (2020) *The Foster Carer's Handbook on Education*, London: CoramBAAF

Bond H (2019) *The Foster Carer's Handbook on Parenting Teenagers*, London: CoramBAAF

Bond H (2021) *Things Foster Carers Need to Know: Young people and gangs*, London: CoramBAAF

Bond H (2021) *Things Foster Carers Need to Know: Young people and self-harm*, London: CoramBAAF

Bond H (2021) *Things Foster Carers Need to Know: Young people and sexuality*, London: CoramBAAF

Fenton K (2019) *Parenting a Child with Toileting Issues*, London: CoramBAAF

Fursland E (2018) *The Adopter's Handbook on Education*, London: CoramBAAF

Parkinson AR (2021) *The Adopter's Handbook on Education (Scotland)*, London: CoramBAAF

Vaughan J and Burnell A (2020) *Parenting a Child with Sleep Issues*, London: CoramBAAF

Vaughan J and Burnell A (2021) *Parenting a Child with Food and Eating Issues*, London: CoramBAAF

Useful organisations

ACE Education
An organisation providing independent advice and information on state education in England to parents and carers.
72 Durnsford Road
London N11 2EJ
Tel: 0300 011 5142 (Mon–Wed 10am–1pm.
Term-time only)
www.ace-ed.org.uk

Action for Children
A charity that supports children, providing practical and emotional care and support.
3 The Boulevard
Ascot Road
Watford WD18 8AG
Tel: 0300 123 2112 (Mon–Fri, 9am–5pm)
www.actionforchildren.org.uk

Anna Freud Centre

An organisation that provides services to families and children with emotional, behavioural and developmental difficulties, and also conducts research into the effectiveness of psychotherapy techniques and children's emotional development.

The Kantor Centre for Excellence
4–8 Rodney Street
London N1 9JH
www.annafreud.org

Book Trust

The UK's largest children's reading charity.
G8 Battersea Studios
80 Silverthorne Road
London SW8 3HE
Tel: 020 7801 8800
www.booktrust.org.uk

CAMHS (Child and Adolescent Mental Health Services)

An NHS service; details can be found on the NHS website.

Caspari Foundation

A charity that helps children overcome emotional, learning and behavioural difficulties. Provides educational psychotherapy to children in some London areas, along with training for school staff.
Finspace
225–229 Seven Sisters Road
London N4 2DA
www.caspari.org.uk

Family Futures

An adoption and fostering agency as well as an assessment and treatment service for traumatised children.
440a Hornsey Road
London N19 4EB
Tel: 020 7354 4161
www.family futures.co.uk

Family Lives

A charity that provides support to family members in all aspects of family life, including parenting, education, running a household, relationships and health.
15–17 The Broadway
Hatfield AL9 5HZ
Tel: 0808 800 2222 (Mon–Fri, 1.30pm–9pm)
www.familylives.org.uk

Kidscape

A London-based charity supporting children affected by bullying by providing practical support, training and advice.
8–10 South Street
Epsom KT18 7PF
Tel: 020 7823 5430
www.kidscape.org.uk

National Bullying Helpline

A help and advice service covering bullying at school and online harassment.
PO Box 1276
Swindon SN25 4UX
Tel: 0300 323 0169 or 0845 2255 787
www.nationalbullyinghelpline.co.uk

National Literacy Trust

An independent charity working with schools and communities to give disadvantaged children literacy skills.

68 South Lambeth Road
London SW8 1RL
Tel: 020 7587 1842
www.literacytrust.org.uk

NSPCC

The UK's leading children's charity.

Weston House
42 Curtain Road
London EC2A 3NH
Tel: 0800 800 5000
www.nspcc.org.uk

PAC–UK (part of Family Action)

A post-adoption support agency that offers a range of support and counselling to adopted children, families and adopted adults.

34 Wharf Road
London N1 7GR
Tel: 020 7284 0555
Advice Line: 0113 230 210
www.pac-uk.org/

PACE (Parents Against Child Exploitation)

An organisation that supports parents and carers whose children are being exploited by offenders outside of the family.

Tel: 0113 240 3040
www.paceuk.info

Parents Protect

An organisation that helps parents and carers protect children from sexual abuse and exploitation.

2 Birch House, Harris Business Park
Hanbury Road
Stoke Prior
Bromsgrove B60 4DJ
Tel: 01527 591922
www.parentsprotect.co.uk

Stonewall

An organisation that provides advice and resources about LGBTQ+ inclusion.

192 St John Street
London EC1V 4JY
Tel: 0800 050 2020
www.stonewall.org.uk

Sutton Trust

An organisation working to improve access to high-quality education and employment opportunities for students from lower income families.

9th floor, Millbank Tower
21–24 Millbank
London SW1P 4QP
Tel: 020 7802 1660
www.suttontrust.com

Tavistock and Portman NHS Foundation Trust

120 Belsize Lane
London NW3 5BA
Tel: 020 7435 7111
www.tavistockandportman.nhs.uk

Fostering, Adoption and Kinship Care Service

An NHS service that provides assessment and treatment for looked after children and young people with emotional and behavioural problems. Details can be found on the Tavistock and Portman NHS Foundation Trust website.

Wise Kids

An organisation that promotes innovative, positive and safe internet use through the provision of training programmes, research, consultancy and resource development.
40 Wood Crescent
Newport NP10 0AL
Tel: 01633 673339
www.wisekids.org.uk

Young Minds

A source of information concerning the mental health of children and families. Publishes leaflets about and for children and young people with mental health problems.
4th floor, India House
Curlew Street
London SE1 2ND
Parents' Helpline: 0808 802 5544
www.youngminds.org.uk

PARENTING MATTERS

This unique series provides expert knowledge about a range of children's health conditions, coupled with facts, figures and guidance presented in a straightforward and accessible style. Adopters and foster carers also describe what it is like to parent an affected child, "telling it like it is", sharing their parenting experiences and offering useful advice.

To find out more visit **www.corambaaf.org.uk/bookshop**